# GED Math Practice Workbook

## 2024

### The Most Comprehensive Review for the Math Section of the GED Test

By

Reza Nazari

All inquiries should be addressed to:
info@effortlessMath.com
www.EffortlessMath.com

**ISBN:** 978-1-63719-023-4

Published by: **Effortless Math Education Inc.**

**For Online Math Practice Visit** www.EffortlessMath.com

# *Welcome to*
# GED Math Prep
## 2024

Thank you for choosing Effortless Math for your GED Math test preparation and congratulations on making the decision to take the GED test! It's a remarkable move you are taking, one that shouldn't be diminished in any capacity.

That's why you need to use every tool possible to ensure you succeed on the test with the highest possible score, and this extensive math workbook is one such tool.

If math has never been a strong subject for you, don't worry! This book along with our online GED Math resources will help you prepare for (and even ACE) the GED Math test. As test day draws nearer, effective preparation becomes increasingly more important. Thankfully, you have this comprehensive workbook to help you get ready for the test. With this book and Effortless Math online resources, you can feel confident that you will be more than ready for the GED Math test when the time comes.

First and foremost, it is important to note that this book is a workbook and not a textbook. Every lesson of this practice book was carefully developed to ensure that you are making the most effective use of your time while preparing for the test. This up-to-date book reflects the 2024 test guidelines and will put you on the right track to hone your math skills, overcome exam anxiety, and boost your confidence, so that you can have your best to succeed on the GED Math test.

**This exercise book will:**

☑ Explain the format of the GED Math test.

☑ Describe specific test-taking strategies that you can use on the test.

☑ Provide GED Math test-taking tips.

☑ Help you identify the areas in which you need to concentrate your study time.

☑ Offer exercises that help you develop the basic math skills you will learn in each section.

☑ Give **2 realistic and full-length practice tests** (featuring new question types) with detailed answers to help you measure your exam readiness and build confidence.

This resource contains comprehensive practice questions and exercises that you will need to prepare for the GED Math test. You'll get numerous skill building exercises as well as tips and techniques on how to prepare for your GED math test.

In addition, in the following pages you'll find:

➢ **How to Use This Book Effectively** – This section provides you with step-by-step instructions on how to get the most out of this comprehensive study guide.

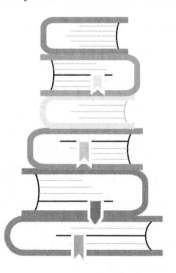

➢ **How to study for the GED Math Test** – A six-step study program has been developed to help you make the best use of this book and prepare for your GED Math test. Here you'll find tips and strategies to guide your study program and help you understand GED Math and how to ace the test.

➢ **GED Math Review** – Learn everything you need to know about the GED Math test.

➢ **GED Math Test-Taking Strategies** – Learn how to effectively put these recommended test-taking techniques into use for improving your GED Math score.

➢ **Test Day Tips** – Review these tips to make sure you will do your best when the big day comes.

## Effortless Math's GED Online Center

Effortless Math Online GED Center offers a complete study program, including the following:

✓ Step-by-step instructions on how to prepare for the GED Math test

✓ Numerous GED Math worksheets to help you measure your math skills

✓ Complete list of GED Math formulas

✓ Video lessons for all GED Math topics

✓ Full-length GED Math practice tests

✓ And much more…

**No Registration Required.**

Visit **EffortlessMath.com/GED** to find your online GED Math resources.

# How to Use This Book Effectively

Look no further when you need a study program to improve your math skills to succeed on the math portion of the GED test. Each chapter of this comprehensive workbook will provide you with the knowledge, tools, and understanding needed for every topic covered on the test.

It's imperative that you understand each topic before moving onto another one, as that's the way to guarantee your success. You can use Effortless Math online course (a free course) to find examples and a step-by-step guide of every math concept in this workbook to better understand the content that will be on the test. To get the best possible results from this book:

> **Begin studying long before your test date**. This provides you ample time to learn the different math concepts. The earlier you begin studying for the test, the sharper your skills will be. Do not procrastinate! Provide yourself with plenty of time to learn the concepts and feel comfortable that you understand them when your test date arrives.

> **Practice consistently**. Study GED Math concepts at least 20 to 30 minutes a day. Remember, slow and steady wins the race, which can be applied to preparing for the GED Math test. Instead of cramming to tackle everything at once, be patient and learn the math topics in short bursts.

> Whenever you get a math problem wrong, **mark it off, and review it later** to make sure you understand the concept.

> Start each session by **looking over the previous material.**

> Once you've reviewed the book's exercises, **take a practice test at the back of the book** to gauge your level of readiness. Then, review your results. Read detailed answers and solutions for each question you missed.

> **Take another practice test** to get an idea of how ready you are to take the actual exam. Taking the practice tests will give you the confidence you need on test day. Simulate the GED testing environment by sitting in a quiet room free from distraction. Make sure to clock yourself with a timer.

# How to Study for the GED Math Test

Studying for the GED Math test can be a really daunting and boring task. What's the best way to go about it? Is there a certain study method that works better than others? Well, studying for the GED Math can be done effectively. The following six-step program has been designed to make preparing for the GED Math test more efficient and less overwhelming.

Step **1** - Create a study plan
Step **2** - Choose your study resources
Step **3** - Review, Learn, Practice
Step **4** - Learn and practice test-taking strategies
Step **5** - Learn the GED Test format and take practice tests
Step **6** - Analyze your performance

## STEP 1: Create a Study Plan

It's always easier to get things done when you have a plan. Creating a study plan for the GED Math test can help you to stay on track with your studies. It's important to sit down and prepare a study plan with what works with your life, work, and any other obligations you may have. Devote enough time each day to studying. It's also a great idea to break down each section of the exam into blocks and study one concept at a time.

It's important to understand that there is no "right" way to create a study plan. Your study plan will be personalized based on your specific needs and learning style.

Follow these guidelines to create an effective study plan for your GED Math test:

★ **Analyze your learning style and study habits** – Everyone has a different learning style. It is essential to embrace your individuality and the unique way you learn. Think about what works and what doesn't work for you. Do you prefer GED Math prep books or a combination of textbooks and video lessons? Does it work better for you if you study every night for thirty minutes or is it more effective to study in the morning before going to work?

★ **Evaluate your schedule** – Review your current schedule and find out how much time you can consistently devote to GED Math study.

★ **Develop a schedule** – Now it's time to add your study schedule to your calendar like any other obligation. Schedule time for study, practice, and review. Plan out which topic you will study on which day to ensure that you're devoting enough time to each concept. Develop a study plan that is mindful, realistic, and flexible.

★ **Stick to your schedule** – A study plan is only effective when it is followed consistently. You should try to develop a study plan that you can follow for the length of your study program.

★ **Evaluate your study plan and adjust as needed** – Sometimes you need to adjust your plan when you have new commitments. Check in with yourself regularly to make sure that you're not falling behind in your study plan. Remember, the most important thing is sticking to your plan. Your study plan is all about helping you be more productive. If you find that your study plan is not as effective as you want, don't get discouraged. It's okay to make changes as you figure out what works best for you.

## STEP 2: Choose Your Study Resources

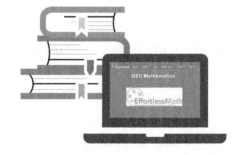

There are numerous textbooks and online resources available for the GED Math test, and it may not be clear where to begin. Don't worry! This exercise book reviews all GED Math concepts and topics. In addition to the book content, you can also use Effortless Math's online resources. (video lessons, worksheets, formulas, etc.) On each page, there is a link (and a QR code) to an online webpage which provides a comprehensive review of the topic, step-by-step instruction, video tutorial, and numerous examples and exercises to help you fully understand the concept.

Simply visit EffortlessMath.com/GED to find your online GED Math resources.

## STEP 3: Review, Learn, Practice

This GED Math exercise book breaks down each subject into specific skills or content areas. For instance, the percent concept is separated into different topics–percent calculation, percent increase and decrease, percent problems, etc. Use this book to help you go over all key math concepts and topics on the GED Math test.

As you review each topic, take notes or highlight the concepts you would like to go over again in the future. If you're unfamiliar with a topic or something is difficult for you, use the link (or the QR code) at the top of the page to find the webpage that provides more instruction about that topic. For each math topic, plenty of instructions, step-by-step guides, and examples are provided to ensure you get a good grasp of the material.

Quickly review the topics you do understand to get a brush-up of the material. Be sure to do the practice questions provided at the end of every chapter to measure your understanding of the concepts.

## STEP 4: Learn and Practice Test-taking Strategies

In the following sections, you will find important test-taking strategies and tips that can help you earn extra points. You'll learn how to think strategically and when to guess if you don't know the answer to a question. Using GED Math test-taking strategies and tips can help you raise your score and do well on the test. Apply test taking strategies on the practice tests to help you boost your confidence.

## STEP 5: Learn the GED Test Format and Take Practice Tests

The *GED Test Review* section provides information about the structure of the GED test. Read this section to learn more about the GED test structure, different test sections, the number of questions in each section, and the section time limits. When you have a prior understanding of the test format and different types of GED Math questions, you'll feel more confident when you take the actual exam.

Once you have read through the instructions and lessons and feel like you are ready to go – take advantage of both of the full-length GED Math practice tests available in this exercise book. Use the practice tests to sharpen your skills and build confidence.

The GED Math practice tests offered at the end of the book are formatted similarly to the actual GED Math test. When you take each practice test, try to simulate actual testing conditions. To take the practice tests, sit in a quiet space, time yourself, and work through as many of the questions as time allows. The practice tests are followed by detailed answer explanations to help you find your weak areas, learn from your mistakes, and raise your GED Math score.

## STEP 6: Analyze Your Performance

After taking the practice tests, look over the answer keys and explanations to learn which questions you answered correctly and which you did not. Never be discouraged if you make a few mistakes. See them as a learning opportunity. This will highlight your strengths and weaknesses.

You can use the results to determine if you need additional practice or if you are ready to take the actual GED Math test.

# Looking for more?

Visit EffortlessMath.com/GED to find hundreds of GED Math worksheets, video tutorials, practice tests, GED Math formulas, and much more.

Or scan this QR code.

**No Registration Required.**

# GED Test Review

T he General Educational Development Test, commonly known as the GED or high school equivalency degree, is a standardized test and is the only high school equivalency test recognized in all 50 USA states.

Currently, the GED is a computer-based test and is given at test centers all over the country. There are four subject area tests on GED:

➤ Reasoning through language arts

➤ Mathematical reasoning

➤ Social studies

➤ Science

**The GED Test at a Glance:**

| Section | Overview | Testing time | Passing Score |
|---|---|---|---|
| Reasoning Through Language Arts | Reading and Writing Skills | 150 minutes | 145 |
| Mathematical Reasoning | Quantitative Math and Algebra | 115 minutes | 145 |
| Science | Life, earth and space, and physical sciences | 90 minutes | 145 |
| Social Studies | Geography, civic, economics, and U.S. history | 90 minutes | 145 |

The GED Mathematical Reasoning test is a 115-minute, single-section test that covers basic mathematics topics, quantitative problem-solving and algebraic questions. There are two parts on the mathematical reasoning section. The first part contains 5 questions and calculators are not permitted. The second part contains 41 questions. A calculator is allowed in the second part. To learn more about how to use the calculator on your GED Math test, visit: EffortlessMath.com/blog/ged-calculator

# GED Math Question Types

The GED Math test has a variety of enhanced question types:

- Multiple-Choice – This is the most common type of question. Multiple-choice questions ask students to choose the one right answer out of four or five possible answer choices.

- Multiple-Select – This type of question is a little different than multiple-choice. Test takers will select all of the correct answer choices among a number of choices. Instead of having just one correct answer, there could be two or more correct answers.

- Fill-in-the-blank – Test takers type their answers in the box, either after a question or in the middle of a sentence. In math, the answer is often numerical but it can sometimes be a word or short phrase.

- Drag-and-Drop – Test takers will need to click and use a "draggable" option to move the answer over to the target region and question it relates to. Sometimes there might be two or more target regions.

- Matching – This question format requires test takers to check a box when data from a column matches the data in a row. True or False questions fall under this question type.

- Table-Entry – This type of question is used when there is a table of values of two columns. Certain cells in the table will have a box where the test taker types in a number to make the table correct.

# How is the GED Scored?

Each GED area test is scored on a scale of 100-200 points. To pass the GED, you must earn at least 145 on each of the four subject tests, for a total of at least 580 points (out of a possible 800).

Each subject test should be passed individually. This means that you must get 145 on each section of the test. If you failed one subject test but did well enough on another to get a total score of 580, that's still not a passing score.

There are four possible scores that you can receive on the GED Test:

**Not Passing**: This indicates that your score is lower than 145 on any of the four tests. If you do not pass, you can reschedule up to two times a year to retake any or all subjects of the GED test.

**Passing Score/High School Equivalency**: This score indicates that your score is between 145-164. Remember that points on one subject of the test do not carry over to the other subjects.

**College Ready**: This indicates that your score is between 165-175, demonstrating career and college readiness. A College Ready score shows that you may not need placement testing or remediation before beginning a college degree program.

**College Ready + Credit**: This indicates that your score is 175 or higher. This shows that you've already mastered some skills that would be taught in college courses. Depending on a school's policy, this can translate to some college credits–saving you time and money during your college education.

# GED Math Test-Taking Strategies

Here are some test-taking strategies that you can use to maximize your performance and results on the GED Math test.

## #1 : USE THIS APPROACH TO ANSWER EVERY GED MATH QUESTION

- Review the question to identify keywords and important information.
- Translate the keywords into math operations so you can solve the problem.
- Review the answer choices. What are the differences between answer choices?
- Draw or label a diagram if needed.
- Try to find patterns.
- Find the right method to answer the question. Use straightforward math, plug in numbers, or test the answer choices (backsolving).
- Double-check your work.

## #2 : USE EDUCATED GUESSING

This approach is applicable to the problems you understand to some degree but cannot solve using straightforward math. In such cases, try to filter out as many answer choices as possible before picking an answer. In cases where you don't have a clue about what a certain problem entails, don't waste any time trying to eliminate answer choices. Just choose one randomly before moving onto the next question.

As you can ascertain, direct solutions are the most optimal approach. Carefully read through the question, determine what the solution is using the math you have learned before, then coordinate the answer with one of the choices available to you. Are you stumped? Make your best guess, then move on.

Don't leave any fields empty! Even if you're unable to work out a problem, strive to answer it. Take a guess if you have to. You will not lose points by getting an answer wrong, though you may gain a point by getting it correct!

# #3: BALLPARK

A ballpark answer is a rough approximation. When we become overwhelmed by calculations and figures, we end up making silly mistakes. A decimal that is moved by one unit can change an answer from right to wrong, regardless of the number of steps that you went through to get it. That's where ballparking can play a big part.

If you think you know what the correct answer may be (even if it's just a ballpark answer), you'll usually have the ability to eliminate a couple of choices. While answer choices are usually based on the average student error and/or values that are closely tied, you will still be able to weed out choices that are way far afield. Try to find answers that aren't in the proverbial ballpark when you're looking for a wrong answer on a multiple-choice question. This is an optimal approach to eliminating answers to a problem.

# #4: BACKSOLVING

A majority of questions on the GED Math test will be in multiple-choice format. Many test-takers prefer multiple-choice questions, as at least the answer is right there. You'll typically have four answers to pick from. You simply need to figure out which one is correct. Usually, the best way to go about doing so is "backsolving."

As mentioned earlier, direct solutions are the most optimal approach to answering a question. Carefully read through a problem, calculate a solution, then correspond the answer with one of the choices displayed in front of you. If you can't calculate a solution, your next best approach involves "backsolving."

When backsolving a problem, contrast one of your answer options against the problem you are asked, then see which of them is most relevant. More often than not, answer choices are listed in ascending or descending order. In such cases, try out the choices B or C. If it's not correct, you can go either down or up from there.

# #5 : PLUGGING IN NUMBERS

"Plugging in numbers" is a strategy that can be applied to a wide range of different math problems on the GED Math test. This approach is typically used to simplify a challenging question so that it is more understandable. By using the strategy carefully, you can find the answer without too much trouble.

The concept is fairly straightforward–replace unknown variables in a problem with certain values. When selecting a number, consider the following:

- Choose a number that's basic (just not too basic). Generally, you should avoid choosing 1 (or even 0). A decent choice is 2.

- Try not to choose a number that is displayed in the problem.

- Make sure you keep your numbers different if you need to choose at least two of them.

- More often than not, choosing numbers merely lets you filter out some of your answer choices. As such, don't just go with the first choice that gives you the right answer.

- If several answers seem correct, then you'll need to choose another value and try again. This time, though, you'll just need to check choices that haven't been eliminated yet.

- If your question contains fractions, then a potential right answer may involve either an LCD (least common denominator) or an LCD multiple.

- 100 is the number you should choose when you are dealing with problems involving percentages.

# GED Math – Test Day Tips

After practicing and reviewing all the math concepts you've been taught, and taking some GED mathematics practice tests, you'll be prepared for test day. Consider the following tips to be extra-ready come test time.

## Before Your Test

What to do the night before:

- **Relax!** One day before your test, study lightly or skip studying altogether. You shouldn't attempt to learn something new, either. There are plenty of reasons why studying the evening before a big test can work against you. Put it this way–a marathoner wouldn't go out for a sprint before the day of a big race. Mental marathoners–such as yourself–should not study for any more than one hour 24 hours before a GED test. That's because your brain requires some rest to be at its best. The night before your exam, spend some time with family or friends, or read a book.

- **Avoid bright screens** - You'll have to get some good shuteye the night before your test. Bright screens (such as the ones coming from your laptop, TV, or mobile device) should be avoided altogether. Staring at such a screen will keep your brain up, making it hard to drift asleep at a reasonable hour.

- **Make sure your dinner is healthy** - The meal that you have for dinner should be nutritious. Be sure to drink plenty of water as well. Load up on your complex carbohydrates, much like a marathon runner would do. Pasta, rice, and potatoes are ideal options here, as are vegetables and protein sources.

- **Get your bag ready for test day** - The night prior to your test, pack your bag with your stationery, admissions pass, ID, and any other gear that you need. Keep the bag right by your front door.

- **Make plans to reach the testing site** - Before going to sleep, ensure that you understand precisely how you will arrive at the site of the test. If parking is something you'll have to find first, plan for it. If you're dependent on public transit, then review the schedule. You should also make sure that the train/bus/subway/streetcar you use will be running. Find out about road closures as well. If a parent or friend is accompanying you, ensure that they understand what steps they have to take as well.

## The Day of the Test ...............................................................................................

- **Get up reasonably early, but not too early.**

- **Have breakfast** - Breakfast improves your concentration, memory, and mood. As such, make sure the breakfast that you eat in the morning is healthy. The last thing you want to be is distracted by a grumbling tummy. If it's not your own stomach making those noises, another test taker close to you might be instead. Prevent discomfort or embarrassment by consuming a healthy breakfast. Bring a snack with you if you think you'll need it.

- **Follow your daily routine** - Do you watch Good Morning America each morning while getting ready for the day? Don't break your usual habits on the day of the test. Likewise, if coffee isn't something you drink in the morning, then don't take up the habit hours before your test. Routine consistency lets you concentrate on the main objective–doing the best you can on your test.

- **Wear layers** - Dress yourself up in comfortable layers. You should be ready for any kind of internal temperature. If it gets too warm during the test, take a layer off.

- **Get there on time** - The last thing you want to do is get to the test site late. Rather, you should be there 45 minutes prior to the start of the test. Upon your arrival, try not to hang out with anybody who is nervous. Any anxious energy they exhibit shouldn't influence you.

- **Leave the books at home** - No books should be brought to the test site. If you start developing anxiety before the test, books could encourage you to do some last-minute studying, which will only hinder you. Keep the books far away–better yet, leave them at home.

- **Make your voice heard** - If something is off, speak to a proctor. If medical attention is needed or if you'll require anything, consult the proctor prior to the start of the test. Any doubts you have should be clarified. You should be entering the test site with a state of mind that is completely clear.

- **Have faith in yourself** - When you feel confident, you will be able to perform at your best. When you are waiting for the test to begin, envision yourself receiving an outstanding result. Try to see yourself as someone who knows all the answers, no matter what the questions are. A lot of athletes tend to use this technique–particularly before a big competition. Your expectations will be reflected by your performance.

## During your test

- **Be calm and breathe deeply** - You need to relax before the test, and some deep breathing will go a long way to help you do that. Be confident and calm. You got this. Everybody feels a little stressed out just before an evaluation of any kind is set to begin. Learn some effective breathing exercises. Spend a minute meditating before the test starts. Filter out any negative thoughts you have. Exhibit confidence when having such thoughts.

- **Concentrate on the test** - Refrain from comparing yourself to anyone else. You shouldn't be distracted by the people near you or random noise. Concentrate exclusively on the test. If you find yourself irritated by surrounding noises, earplugs can be used to block sounds off close to you. Don't forget–the test is going to last several hours if you're taking more than one subject of the test. Some of that time will be dedicated to brief sections. Concentrate on the specific section you are working on during a particular moment. Do not let your mind wander off to upcoming or previous sections.

- **Skip challenging questions** - Optimize your time when taking the test. Lingering on a single question for too long will work against you. If you don't know what the answer is to a certain question, use your best guess, and mark the question so you can review it later on. There is no need to spend time attempting to solve something you aren't sure about. That time would be better served handling the questions you can actually answer well. You will not be penalized for getting the wrong answer on a test like this.

- **Try to answer each question individually** - Focus only on the question you are working on. Use one of the test-taking strategies to solve the problem. If you aren't able to come up with an answer, don't get frustrated. Simply skip that question, then move onto the next one.

■ **Don't forget to breathe!** Whenever you notice your mind wandering, your stress levels boosting, or frustration brewing, take a thirty-second break. Shut your eyes, drop your pencil, breathe deeply, and let your shoulders relax. You will end up being more productive when you allow yourself to relax for a moment.

■ **Review your answer.** If you still have time at the end of the test, don't waste it. Go back and check over your answers. It is worth going through the test from start to finish to ensure that you didn't make a sloppy mistake somewhere.

■ **Optimize your breaks** - When break time comes, use the restroom, have a snack, and reactivate your energy for the subsequent section. Doing some stretches can help stimulate your blood flow.

## After your test

■ **Take it easy** - You will need to set some time aside to relax and decompress once the test has concluded. There is no need to stress yourself out about what you could've said, or what you may have done wrong. At this point, there's nothing you can do about it. Your energy and time would be better spent on something that will bring you happiness for the remainder of your day.

■ **Redoing the test** - Did you pass the test? Congratulations! Your hard work paid off! Passing this test means that you are now as knowledgeable as somebody who has graduated high school.

If you have failed your test, though, don't worry! The test can be retaken. In such cases, you will need to follow the retake policy established by your state. You also need to re-register to take the exam again.

# Contents

# Contents

# Contents

# Chapter 1: Fractions and Mixed Numbers

**Math Topics that you'll learn in this Chapter:**

- ✓ Simplifying Fractions
- ✓ Adding and Subtracting Fractions
- ✓ Multiplying and Dividing Fractions
- ✓ Adding Mixed Numbers
- ✓ Subtracting Mixed Numbers
- ✓ Multiplying Mixed Numbers
- ✓ Dividing Mixed Numbers

1

## Simplifying Fractions

✍ *Simplify each fraction.*

1) $\frac{8}{16} =$

2) $\frac{7}{21} =$

3) $\frac{11}{44} =$

4) $\frac{6}{24} =$

5) $\frac{6}{18} =$

6) $\frac{18}{27} =$

7) $\frac{15}{55} =$

8) $\frac{24}{54} =$

9) $\frac{63}{72} =$

10) $\frac{40}{64} =$

11) $\frac{23}{46} =$

12) $\frac{35}{63} =$

13) $\frac{32}{36} =$

14) $\frac{81}{99} =$

15) $\frac{16}{64} =$

16) $\frac{14}{35} =$

17) $\frac{19}{38} =$

18) $\frac{18}{54} =$

19) $\frac{56}{70} =$

20) $\frac{40}{45} =$

21) $\frac{9}{90} =$

22) $\frac{20}{25} =$

23) $\frac{36}{42} =$

24) $\frac{40}{48} =$

25) $\frac{18}{54} =$

26) $\frac{48}{144} =$

# Adding and Subtracting Fractions

✎ *Calculate and write the answer in lowest term.*

1) $\frac{1}{3} + \frac{1}{5} =$

2) $\frac{2}{5} + \frac{3}{8} =$

3) $\frac{1}{3} - \frac{2}{9} =$

4) $\frac{4}{5} - \frac{2}{9} =$

5) $\frac{2}{9} + \frac{1}{3} =$

6) $\frac{3}{10} + \frac{2}{5} =$

7) $\frac{9}{10} - \frac{4}{5} =$

8) $\frac{7}{9} - \frac{3}{7} =$

9) $\frac{3}{4} + \frac{1}{3} =$

10) $\frac{3}{8} + \frac{2}{5} =$

11) $\frac{3}{4} - \frac{2}{5} =$

12) $\frac{7}{9} - \frac{2}{3} =$

13) $\frac{4}{9} + \frac{5}{6} =$

14) $\frac{2}{3} + \frac{1}{4} =$

15) $\frac{9}{10} - \frac{3}{5} =$

16) $\frac{7}{12} - \frac{1}{2} =$

17) $\frac{4}{5} + \frac{2}{3} =$

18) $\frac{5}{7} + \frac{1}{5} =$

19) $\frac{5}{9} - \frac{2}{5} =$

20) $\frac{3}{5} - \frac{2}{9} =$

21) $\frac{7}{9} + \frac{1}{7} =$

22) $\frac{5}{8} + \frac{2}{3} =$

23) $\frac{5}{7} - \frac{2}{5} =$

24) $\frac{7}{9} - \frac{3}{4} =$

25) $\frac{3}{5} - \frac{1}{6} =$

26) $\frac{3}{12} + \frac{2}{7} =$

# Multiplying and Dividing Fractions

✍ *Solve and write the answer in lowest term.*

1) $\frac{1}{3} \times \frac{9}{5} =$

2) $\frac{1}{4} \times \frac{3}{7} =$

3) $\frac{1}{5} \div \frac{1}{4} =$

4) $\frac{1}{6} \div \frac{5}{12} =$

5) $\frac{2}{3} \times \frac{4}{7} =$

6) $\frac{5}{7} \times \frac{3}{4} =$

7) $\frac{2}{5} \div \frac{3}{7} =$

8) $\frac{3}{7} \div \frac{5}{8} =$

9) $\frac{3}{8} \times \frac{4}{7} =$

10) $\frac{2}{9} \times \frac{6}{11} =$

11) $\frac{1}{10} \div \frac{3}{8} =$

12) $\frac{3}{10} \div \frac{4}{5} =$

13) $\frac{6}{7} \times \frac{4}{9} =$

14) $\frac{3}{7} \times \frac{5}{6} =$

15) $\frac{7}{9} \div \frac{6}{11} =$

16) $\frac{1}{15} \div \frac{2}{3} =$

17) $\frac{1}{13} \times \frac{1}{2} =$

18) $\frac{1}{12} \times \frac{4}{7} =$

19) $\frac{1}{15} \div \frac{4}{9} =$

20) $\frac{1}{16} \div \frac{1}{2} =$

21) $\frac{4}{7} \times \frac{5}{8} =$

22) $\frac{1}{11} \times \frac{4}{5} =$

23) $\frac{1}{16} \div \frac{5}{8} =$

24) $\frac{1}{15} \div \frac{2}{3} =$

25) $\frac{1}{13} \times \frac{2}{5} =$

26) $\frac{1}{18} \times \frac{3}{7} =$

## Adding Mixed Numbers

✐ *Solve and write the answer in lowest terms.*

1) $1\frac{1}{5} + 2\frac{2}{5} =$

2) $1\frac{1}{2} + 4\frac{5}{6} =$

3) $2\frac{4}{5} + 2\frac{3}{10} =$

4) $3\frac{1}{6} + 2\frac{2}{5} =$

5) $1\frac{5}{6} + 1\frac{2}{5} =$

6) $3\frac{5}{7} + 1\frac{2}{9} =$

7) $3\frac{5}{8} + 2\frac{1}{3} =$

8) $1\frac{6}{7} + 3\frac{2}{9} =$

9) $2\frac{5}{9} + 1\frac{1}{4} =$

10) $3\frac{7}{9} + 2\frac{5}{6} =$

11) $2\frac{1}{10} + 2\frac{2}{5} =$

12) $1\frac{3}{10} + 3\frac{4}{5} =$

13) $3\frac{1}{12} + 2\frac{1}{3} =$

14) $5\frac{1}{11} + 1\frac{1}{2} =$

15) $3\frac{1}{21} + 2\frac{2}{3} =$

16) $4\frac{1}{24} + 1\frac{5}{8} =$

17) $2\frac{1}{25} + 3\frac{3}{5} =$

18) $3\frac{1}{15} + 2\frac{2}{10} =$

19) $5\frac{6}{7} + 2\frac{1}{3} =$

20) $2\frac{1}{8} + 3\frac{3}{4} =$

21) $2\frac{5}{7} + 2\frac{2}{21} =$

22) $4\frac{1}{6} + 1\frac{4}{5} =$

23) $2\frac{1}{7} + 2\frac{3}{8} =$

24) $3\frac{1}{4} + 2\frac{2}{3} =$

25) $1\frac{1}{13} + 2\frac{3}{4} =$

26) $3\frac{2}{35} + 2\frac{5}{7} =$

Chapter 1: Fractions and Mixed Numbers

## Subtracting Mixed Numbers

✐ *Solve and write the answer in lowest terms.*

1) $5\frac{2}{9} - 2\frac{1}{9} =$

2) $6\frac{2}{7} - 2\frac{1}{3} =$

3) $5\frac{3}{8} - 2\frac{3}{4} =$

4) $7\frac{2}{5} - 3\frac{1}{10} =$

5) $9\frac{5}{7} - 7\frac{4}{21} =$

6) $11\frac{7}{12} - 9\frac{5}{6} =$

7) $9\frac{5}{9} - 8\frac{1}{8} =$

8) $13\frac{7}{9} - 11\frac{3}{7} =$

9) $8\frac{7}{12} - 7\frac{3}{8} =$

10) $11\frac{5}{9} - 9\frac{1}{4} =$

11) $6\frac{5}{6} - 2\frac{2}{9} =$

12) $5\frac{7}{8} - 4\frac{1}{3} =$

13) $9\frac{5}{8} - 8\frac{1}{2} =$

14) $4\frac{9}{16} - 2\frac{1}{4} =$

15) $3\frac{2}{3} - 1\frac{2}{15} =$

16) $5\frac{1}{2} - 4\frac{2}{17} =$

17) $5\frac{6}{7} - 2\frac{1}{3} =$

18) $3\frac{3}{7} - 2\frac{2}{21} =$

19) $7\frac{3}{10} - 5\frac{2}{15} =$

20) $4\frac{5}{6} - 2\frac{2}{9} =$

21) $6\frac{3}{7} - 2\frac{2}{9} =$

22) $7\frac{4}{5} - 6\frac{3}{7} =$

23) $12\frac{3}{7} - 8\frac{1}{3} =$

24) $5\frac{4}{9} - 2\frac{5}{6} =$

25) $10\frac{1}{28} - 7\frac{3}{4} =$

26) $11\frac{5}{12} - 7\frac{5}{48} =$

## Multiplying Mixed Numbers

✎ *Solve and write the answer in lowest terms.*

1) $1\frac{1}{6} \times 1\frac{3}{7} =$

2) $5\frac{1}{6} \times 2\frac{1}{4} =$

3) $3\frac{3}{7} \times 1\frac{2}{9} =$

4) $3\frac{3}{8} \times 3\frac{1}{6} =$

5) $1\frac{1}{2} \times 5\frac{2}{3} =$

6) $3\frac{1}{2} \times 6\frac{2}{3} =$

7) $9\frac{1}{2} \times 2\frac{1}{6} =$

8) $2\frac{5}{8} \times 8\frac{3}{5} =$

9) $3\frac{4}{5} \times 4\frac{2}{3} =$

10) $5\frac{1}{3} \times 2\frac{2}{7} =$

11) $6\frac{1}{3} \times 3\frac{3}{4} =$

12) $7\frac{2}{3} \times 1\frac{8}{9} =$

13) $8\frac{1}{2} \times 2\frac{1}{6} =$

14) $4\frac{1}{5} \times 8\frac{2}{3} =$

15) $3\frac{1}{8} \times 5\frac{2}{3} =$

16) $2\frac{2}{7} \times 6\frac{2}{5} =$

17) $2\frac{3}{8} \times 7\frac{2}{3} =$

18) $1\frac{7}{8} \times 8\frac{2}{3} =$

19) $9\frac{1}{2} \times 3\frac{1}{5} =$

20) $2\frac{5}{8} \times 4\frac{1}{3} =$

21) $6\frac{1}{3} \times 3\frac{2}{5} =$

22) $5\frac{3}{4} \times 2\frac{2}{7} =$

23) $8\frac{1}{6} \times 2\frac{2}{7} =$

24) $4\frac{1}{6} \times 7\frac{1}{5} =$

25) $2\frac{1}{5} \times 2\frac{5}{8} =$

26) $6\frac{2}{3} \times 4\frac{3}{5} =$

## Dividing Mixed Numbers

✏️ *Solve and write the answer in lowest terms.*

1) $6\frac{1}{2} \div 4\frac{2}{5} =$

2) $1\frac{3}{8} \div 1\frac{1}{4} =$

3) $6\frac{2}{5} \div 2\frac{4}{5} =$

4) $7\frac{1}{3} \div 6\frac{3}{4} =$

5) $7\frac{2}{5} \div 3\frac{3}{4} =$

6) $2\frac{4}{5} \div 3\frac{2}{3} =$

7) $8\frac{3}{5} \div 4\frac{3}{4} =$

8) $6\frac{3}{4} \div 2\frac{2}{9} =$

9) $5\frac{2}{7} \div 2\frac{2}{9} =$

10) $2\frac{2}{5} \div 3\frac{3}{5} =$

11) $4\frac{3}{7} \div 1\frac{7}{8} =$

12) $2\frac{5}{7} \div 2\frac{4}{5} =$

13) $8\frac{3}{5} \div 6\frac{1}{5} =$

14) $2\frac{5}{8} \div 1\frac{8}{9} =$

15) $5\frac{6}{7} \div 2\frac{3}{4} =$

16) $1\frac{3}{5} \div 2\frac{3}{8} =$

17) $5\frac{3}{4} \div 3\frac{2}{5} =$

18) $2\frac{3}{4} \div 3\frac{1}{5} =$

19) $3\frac{2}{3} \div 1\frac{2}{5} =$

20) $4\frac{1}{4} \div 2\frac{2}{3} =$

21) $3\frac{5}{6} \div 2\frac{4}{5} =$

22) $2\frac{1}{8} \div 1\frac{3}{4} =$

23) $5\frac{1}{2} \div 4\frac{2}{5} =$

24) $6\frac{3}{7} \div 2\frac{1}{7} =$

25) $3\frac{3}{6} \div 1\frac{5}{7} =$

26) $4\frac{4}{9} \div 4\frac{2}{3} =$

# Answers – Chapter 1

## Simplifying Fractions

1) $\frac{1}{2}$

2) $\frac{1}{3}$

3) $\frac{1}{4}$

4) $\frac{1}{4}$

5) $\frac{1}{3}$

6) $\frac{2}{3}$

7) $\frac{3}{11}$

8) $\frac{4}{9}$

9) $\frac{7}{8}$

10) $\frac{5}{8}$

11) $\frac{1}{2}$

12) $\frac{5}{9}$

13) $\frac{8}{9}$

14) $\frac{9}{11}$

15) $\frac{1}{4}$

16) $\frac{2}{5}$

17) $\frac{1}{2}$

18) $\frac{1}{3}$

19) $\frac{4}{5}$

20) $\frac{8}{9}$

21) $\frac{1}{10}$

22) $\frac{4}{5}$

23) $\frac{6}{7}$

24) $\frac{5}{6}$

25) $\frac{1}{3}$

26) $\frac{1}{3}$

## Adding and Subtracting Fractions

1) $\frac{8}{15}$

2) $\frac{31}{40}$

3) $\frac{1}{9}$

4) $\frac{26}{45}$

5) $\frac{5}{9}$

6) $\frac{7}{10}$

7) $\frac{1}{10}$

8) $\frac{22}{63}$

9) $\frac{13}{12}$

10) $\frac{31}{40}$

11) $\frac{7}{20}$

12) $\frac{1}{9}$

13) $\frac{23}{18}$

14) $\frac{11}{12}$

15) $\frac{3}{10}$

16) $\frac{1}{12}$

17) $\frac{22}{15}$

18) $\frac{32}{35}$

19) $\frac{7}{45}$

20) $\frac{17}{45}$

21) $\frac{58}{63}$

22) $\frac{31}{24}$

23) $\frac{11}{35}$

24) $\frac{1}{36}$

25) $\frac{13}{30}$

26) $\frac{15}{28}$

## Multiplying and Dividing Fractions

1) $\frac{3}{5}$

2) $\frac{3}{28}$

3) $\frac{4}{5}$

4) $\frac{2}{5}$

5) $\frac{8}{21}$

6) $\frac{15}{28}$

7) $\frac{14}{15}$

8) $\frac{24}{35}$

9) $\frac{3}{14}$

10) $\frac{4}{33}$

11) $\frac{4}{15}$

12) $\frac{3}{8}$

13) $\frac{8}{21}$

14) $\frac{5}{14}$

15) $\frac{77}{54}$

16) $\frac{1}{10}$

17) $\frac{1}{26}$

18) $\frac{1}{21}$

19) $\frac{3}{20}$

20) $\frac{1}{8}$

21) $\frac{5}{14}$

22) $\frac{4}{55}$

23) $\frac{1}{10}$

24) $\frac{1}{10}$

25) $\frac{2}{65}$

26) $\frac{1}{42}$

## Adding Mixed Numbers

1) $3\frac{3}{5}$

2) $6\frac{1}{3}$

3) $5\frac{1}{10}$

4) $5\frac{17}{30}$

5) $3\frac{7}{30}$

6) $4\frac{59}{63}$

7) $5\frac{23}{24}$

8) $5\frac{5}{63}$

9) $3\frac{29}{36}$

10) $6\frac{11}{18}$

11) $4\frac{1}{2}$

12) $5\frac{1}{10}$

13) $5\frac{5}{12}$

14) $6\frac{13}{22}$

15) $5\frac{5}{7}$

16) $5\frac{2}{3}$

17) $5\frac{16}{25}$

18) $5\frac{4}{15}$

19) $8\frac{4}{21}$

20) $5\frac{7}{8}$

21) $4\frac{17}{21}$

22) $5\frac{29}{30}$

23) $4\frac{29}{56}$

24) $5\frac{11}{12}$

25) $3\frac{43}{52}$

26) $5\frac{27}{35}$

## Subtracting Mixed Numbers

1) $3\frac{1}{9}$

2) $3\frac{20}{21}$

3) $2\frac{5}{8}$

4) $4\frac{3}{10}$

5) $2\frac{11}{21}$

6) $1\frac{3}{4}$

7) $1\frac{31}{72}$

8) $2\frac{22}{63}$

9) $1\frac{5}{24}$

10) $2\frac{11}{36}$

11) $4\frac{11}{18}$

12) $1\frac{13}{24}$

13) $1\frac{1}{8}$

14) $2\frac{5}{16}$

15) $2\frac{8}{15}$

16) $1\frac{13}{34}$

17) $3\frac{11}{21}$

18) $1\frac{1}{3}$

19) $2\frac{1}{6}$

20) $2\frac{11}{18}$

21) $4\frac{13}{63}$

22) $1\frac{13}{35}$

23) $4\frac{2}{21}$

24) $2\frac{11}{18}$

25) $2\frac{2}{7}$

26) $4\frac{5}{16}$

## Multiplying Mixed Numbers

1) $1\frac{2}{3}$

2) $11\frac{5}{8}$

3) $4\frac{4}{21}$

4) $10\frac{11}{16}$

5) $8\frac{1}{2}$

6) $23\frac{1}{3}$

7) $20\frac{7}{12}$

8) $22\frac{23}{40}$

9) $17\frac{11}{15}$

10) $12\frac{4}{21}$

11) $23\frac{3}{4}$

12) $14\frac{13}{27}$

13) $18\frac{5}{12}$

14) $36\frac{2}{5}$

15) $17\frac{17}{24}$

16) $14\frac{22}{35}$

17) $18\frac{5}{24}$

18) $16\frac{1}{4}$

19) $30\frac{2}{5}$

20) $11\frac{3}{8}$

21) $21\frac{8}{15}$

22) $13\frac{1}{7}$

23) $18\frac{2}{3}$

24) $30$

25) $5\frac{31}{40}$

26) $30\frac{2}{3}$

## Dividing Mixed Numbers

1) $1\frac{21}{44}$

2) $1\frac{1}{10}$

3) $2\frac{2}{7}$

4) $1\frac{7}{81}$

5) $1\frac{73}{75}$

6) $\frac{42}{55}$

7) $1\frac{77}{95}$

8) $3\frac{3}{80}$

9) $2\frac{53}{140}$

10) $\frac{2}{3}$

11) $2\frac{88}{105}$

12) $\frac{95}{98}$

13) $1\frac{12}{31}$

14) $1\frac{53}{136}$

15) $2\frac{10}{77}$

16) $\frac{64}{95}$

17) $1\frac{47}{68}$

18) $\frac{55}{64}$

19) $2\frac{13}{21}$

20) $1\frac{19}{32}$

21) $1\frac{31}{84}$

22) $1\frac{3}{14}$

23) $1\frac{1}{4}$

24) $3$

25) $2\frac{1}{24}$

26) $\frac{20}{21}$

# Chapter 2: Decimal

**Math Topics that you'll learn in this Chapter:**

- ✓ Comparing Decimals
- ✓ Rounding Decimals
- ✓ Adding and Subtracting Decimals
- ✓ Multiplying and Dividing Decimals

13

## Comparing Decimals

✎ *Compare. Use* >, =, *and* <

1) 0.44 ☐ 0.044

2) 0.67 ☐ 0.68

3) 0.49 ☐ 0.79

4) 1.35 ☐ 1.45

5) 1.58 ☐ 1.75

6) 2.91 ☐ 2.85

7) 14.56 ☐ 1.456

8) 17.85 ☐ 17.89

9) 21.52 ☐ 21.052

10) 11.12 ☐ 11.03

11) 9.650 ☐ 9.65

12) 8.578 ☐ 8.568

13) 3.15 ☐ 0.315

14) 16.61 ☐ 16.16

15) 18.581 ☐ 8.991

16) 25.05 ☐ 2.505

17) 4.55 ☐ 4.65

18) 0.158 ☐ 1.58

19) 0.881 ☐ 0.871

20) 0.505 ☐ 0.510

21) 0.772 ☐ 0.777

22) 0.5 ☐ 0.500

23) 16.89 ☐ 15.89

24) 12.25 ☐ 12.35

25) 5.82 ☐ 5.69

26) 1.320 ☐ 1.032

27) 0.082 ☐ 0.088

28) 0.99 ☐ 0.099

29) 2.360 ☐ 2.840

30) 0.330 ☐ 0.303

31) 16.44 ☐ 1.664

32) 0.424 ☐ 0.442

## Rounding Decimals

✍ *Round each number to the underlined place value.*

1) $\underline{3}.960 =$

2) $4.3\underline{7}2 =$

3) $11.13\underline{6} =$

4) $1\underline{7}.5 =$

5) $1.9\underline{8}1 =$

6) $14.\underline{2}15 =$

7) $17.5\underline{4}8 =$

8) $25.5\underline{0}8 =$

9) $3\underline{1}.089 =$

10) $69.\underline{3}45 =$

11) $9.4\underline{5}7 =$

12) $1\underline{2}.901 =$

13) $2.6\underline{5}8 =$

14) $32.\underline{5}65 =$

15) $6.0\underline{5}8 =$

16) $98.1\underline{0}8 =$

17) $27.\underline{7}05 =$

18) $3\underline{6}.75 =$

19) $9.\underline{0}8 =$

20) $7.\underline{1}85 =$

21) $22.5\underline{4}7 =$

22) $66.\underline{0}98 =$

23) $8\underline{7}.75 =$

24) $18.\underline{5}41 =$

25) $10.2\underline{5}8 =$

26) $13.\underline{4}56 =$

27) $71.0\underline{8}4 =$

28) $2\underline{9}.23 =$

29) $43.\underline{4}5 =$

30) $8\underline{1}.07 =$

31) $9\underline{2}.366 =$

32) $24.\underline{7}6 =$

Chapter 2: Decimal

## Adding and Subtracting Decimals

✎ *Solve.*

1) $11.62 + 18.23 =$

2) $13.78 + 16.58 =$

3) $56.30 - 45.68 =$

4) $59.36 - 30.88 =$

5) $24.32 + 26.45 =$

6) $36.25 + 18.37 =$

7) $47.85 - 35.12 =$

8) $85.65 - 67.48 =$

9) $25.49 + 34.18 =$

10) $19.99 + 48.66 =$

11) $46.32 - 27.77 =$

12) $54.62 - 48.12 =$

13) $24.42 + 16.54 =$

14) $52.13 + 12.32 =$

15) $82.36 - 78.65 =$

16) $64.12 - 49.15 =$

17) $36.41 + 24.52 =$

18) $85.96 - 74.63 =$

19) $52.62 - 42.54 =$

20) $21.20 + 24.58 =$

21) $32.15 + 17.17 =$

22) $96.32 - 85.54 =$

23) $89.78 - 69.85 =$

24) $29.28 + 39.79 =$

25) $11.11 + 19.99 =$

26) $28.82 + 20.88 =$

27) $63.14 - 28.91 =$

28) $56.61 - 49.72 =$

29) $66.14 + 32.12 =$

30) $30.19 + 25.83 =$

31) $68.21 - 25.10 =$

32) $76.57 - 45.13 =$

# Multiplying and Dividing Decimals

✎ **Solve.**

1) $12.3 \times 0.2 =$

2) $12.6 \times 0.9 =$

3) $54.4 \div 2 =$

4) $64.8 \div 8 =$

5) $23.1 \times 0.3 =$

6) $1.2 \times 0.7 =$

7) $5.5 \div 0.5 =$

8) $64.8 \div 8 =$

9) $1.4 \times 0.5 =$

10) $4.5 \times 0.3 =$

11) $88.8 \div 4 =$

12) $10.5 \div 5 =$

13) $2.2 \times 0.3 =$

14) $0.2 \times 0.52 =$

15) $95.7 \div 100 =$

16) $36.6 \div 6 =$

17) $3.2 \times 2 =$

18) $4.1 \times 0.5 =$

19) $68.4 \div 2 =$

20) $27.9 \div 9 =$

21) $3.5 \times 4 =$

22) $4.8 \times 0.5 =$

23) $6.4 \div 4 =$

24) $72.8 \div 0.8 =$

25) $1.8 \times 3 =$

26) $6.5 \times 0.2 =$

27) $93.6 \div 3 =$

28) $45.15 \div 0.5 =$

29) $12.6 \times 0.5 =$

30) $13.2 \times 6 =$

31) $6.4 \div 0.8 =$

32) $98.6 \div 0.2 =$

# Answers – Chapter 2

**Comparing Decimals**

1) $0.44 > 0.044$

2) $0.67 < 0.68$

3) $0.49 < 0.79$

4) $1.35 < 1.45$

5) $1.58 < 1.75$

6) $2.91 > 2.85$

7) $14.56 > 1.456$

8) $17.85 < 17.89$

9) $21.52 > 21.052$

10) $11.12 > 11.03$

11) $9.650 = 9.65$

12) $8.578 > 8.568$

13) $3.15 > 0.315$

14) $16.61 > 16.16$

15) $18.581 > 8.991$

16) $25.05 > 2.505$

17) $4.55 < 4.65$

18) $0.158 < 1.58$

19) $0.881 > 0.871$

20) $0.505 < 0.510$

21) $0.772 < 0.777$

22) $0.5 = 0.500$

23) $16.89 > 15.89$

24) $12.25 < 12.35$

25) $5.82 > 5.69$

26) $1.320 > 1.032$

27) $0.082 < 0.088$

28) $0.99 > 0.099$

29) $2.360 < 2.840$

30) $0.330 > 0.303$

31) $16.44 > 1.664$

32) $0.424 < 0.442$

## Rounding Decimals

1) $\underline{3}.960 = 4$

2) $4.3\underline{7}2 = 4.37$

3) $11.1\underline{3}6 = 11.14$

4) $1\underline{7}.5 = 18$

5) $1.9\underline{8}1 = 1.98$

6) $14.\underline{2}15 = 14.2$

7) $17.5\underline{4}8 = 17.55$

8) $25.5\underline{0}8 = 25.51$

9) $3\underline{1}.089 = 31$

10) $69.\underline{3}45 = 69.3$

11) $9.4\underline{5}7 = 9.46$

12) $1\underline{2}.901 = 13$

13) $2.6\underline{5}8 = 2.66$

14) $32.\underline{5}65 = 32.6$

15) $6.0\underline{5}8 = 6.06$

16) $98.1\underline{0}8 = 98.11$

17) $27.\underline{7}05 = 27.7$

18) $3\underline{6}.75 = 37$

19) $9.\underline{0}8 = 9.1$

20) $7.\underline{1}85 = 7.2$

21) $22.5\underline{4}7 = 22.55$

22) $66.\underline{0}98 = 66.1$

23) $8\underline{7}.75 = 88$

24) $18.\underline{5}41 = 18.5$

25) $10.2\underline{5}8 = 10.26$

26) $13.\underline{4}56 = 13.5$

27) $71.0\underline{8}4 = 71.08$

28) $2\underline{9}.23 = 29$

29) $43.\underline{4}5 = 43.5$

30) $8\underline{1}.07 = 81$

31) $9\underline{2}.366 = 92$

32) $24.\underline{7}6 = 24.8$

## Adding and Subtracting Decimals

| | | | |
|---|---|---|---|
| 1) 29.85 | 9) 59.67 | 17) 60.93 | 25) 31.1 |
| 2) 30.36 | 10) 68.65 | 18) 11.33 | 26) 49.7 |
| 3) 10.62 | 11) 18.55 | 19) 10.08 | 27) 34.23 |
| 4) 28.48 | 12) 6.5 | 20) 45.78 | 28) 6.89 |
| 5) 50.77 | 13) 40.96 | 21) 49.32 | 29) 98.26 |
| 6) 54.62 | 14) 64.45 | 22) 10.78 | 30) 56.02 |
| 7) 12.73 | 15) 3.71 | 23) 19.93 | 31) 43.11 |
| 8) 18.17 | 16) 14.97 | 24) 69.07 | 32) 31.44 |

## Multiplying and Dividing Decimals

| | | | |
|---|---|---|---|
| 1) 2.46 | 9) 0.7 | 17) 6.4 | 25) 5.4 |
| 2) 11.34 | 10) 1.35 | 18) 2.05 | 26) 1.3 |
| 3) 27.2 | 11) 22.2 | 19) 34.2 | 27) 31.2 |
| 4) 8.1 | 12) 2.1 | 20) 3.1 | 28) 90.3 |
| 5) 6.93 | 13) 0.66 | 21) 14 | 29) 6.3 |
| 6) 0.84 | 14) 0.104 | 22) 2.4 | 30) 79.2 |
| 7) 11 | 15) 0.957 | 23) 1.6 | 31) 8 |
| 8) 8.1 | 16) 6.1 | 24) 91 | 32) 493 |

# Chapter 3: Integers and Order of Operations

**Math Topics that you'll learn in this Chapter:**

- ✓ Adding and Subtracting Integers
- ✓ Multiplying and Dividing Integers
- ✓ Order of Operations
- ✓ Integers and Absolute Value

## Adding and Subtracting Integers

✎ *Solve.*

1) $-(9) + 15 =$

2) $15 - (-11 - 9) =$

3) $(-10) + (-6) =$

4) $(-10) + (-6) + 7 =$

5) $-(23) + 19 =$

6) $(-7 + 5) - 9 =$

7) $28 + (-32) =$

8) $(-11) + (-9) + 5 =$

9) $25 - (8 - 7) =$

10) $-(29) + 17 =$

11) $(-38) + (-3) + 29 =$

12) $15 - (-7 + 9) =$

13) $24 - (8 - 2) =$

14) $(-7 + 4) - 9 =$

15) $(-17) + (-3) + 9 =$

16) $(-26) + (-7) + 8 =$

17) $(-9) + (-11) =$

18) $8 - (-23 - 13) =$

19) $(-16) + (-2) =$

20) $25 - (7 - 4) =$

21) $23 + (-12) =$

22) $(-18) + (-6) =$

23) $17 - (-21 - 7) =$

24) $-(28) - (-16) + 5 =$

25) $(-9 + 4) - 8 =$

26) $(-28) + (-6) + 17 =$

27) $-(21) - (-15) + 9 =$

28) $(-31) + (-6) =$

29) $(-18) + (-10) + 13 =$

30) $(-30) + (-11) + 12 =$

31) $-(28) - (-10) + 6 =$

32) $6 - (-16 - 11) =$

# Multiplying and Dividing Integers

✏️ *Solve.*

1) $(-6) \times (-7) =$

2) $8 \times (-5) =$

3) $48 \div (-8) =$

4) $(-72) \div 9 =$

5) $(4) \times (-6) =$

6) $(-9) \times (-11) =$

7) $(10) \div (-5) =$

8) $144 \div (-12) =$

9) $(10) \times (-2) =$

10) $(-8) \times (-2) \times 5 =$

11) $(8) \div (-2) =$

12) $45 \div (-15) =$

13) $(5) \times (-7) =$

14) $(-6) \times (-5) \times 4 =$

15) $(12) \div (-6) =$

16) $(14) \div (-7) =$

17) $196 \div (-14) =$

18) $(27 - 13) \times (-2) =$

19) $125 \div (-5) =$

20) $66 \div (-6) =$

21) $(-6) \times (-5) \times 3 =$

22) $(15 - 6) \times (-3) =$

23) $(32 - 24) \div (-4) =$

24) $72 \div (-6) =$

25) $(-14 + 8) \times (-7) =$

26) $(-3) \times (-9) \times 3 =$

27) $84 \div (-12) =$

28) $(-12) \times (-10) =$

29) $22 \times (-3) =$

30) $(-2) \times (-6) \times 5 =$

31) $(24) \div (-3) =$

32) $(-15) \div (3) =$

## Order of Operation

✎ *Calculate.*

1) $16 + (30 \div 5) =$

2) $(3 \times 9) \div (-3) =$

3) $57 - (3 \times 8) =$

4) $(-12) \times (7 - 3) =$

5) $(18 - 7) \times (6) =$

6) $(6 \times 10) \div (12 + 3) =$

7) $(13 \times 2) - (24 \div 6) =$

8) $(-5) + (4 \times 3) + 8 =$

9) $(4 \times 2^3) + (16 - 9) =$

10) $(3^2 \times 7) \div (-2 + 1) =$

11) $[-2(48 \div 2^3)] - 6 =$

12) $(-4) + (7 \times 8) + 18 =$

13) $(3 \times 7) + (16 - 7) =$

14) $[3^3 \times (48 \div 2^3)] \div (-2) =$

15) $(14 \times 3) - (3^4 \div 9) =$

16) $(96 \div 12) \times (-3) =$

17) $(48 \div 2^2) \times (-2) =$

18) $(56 \div 7) \times (-5) =$

19) $(-2^2) + (7 \times 9) - 21 =$

20) $(2^4 - 9) \times (-6) =$

21) $[4^3 \times (50 \div 5^2)] \div (-16) =$

22) $(3^2 \times 4^2) \div (-4 + 2) =$

23) $6^2 - (-6 \times 4) + 3 =$

24) $4^2 - (5^2 \times 3) =$

25) $(-4) + (12^2 \div 3^2) - 7^2 =$

26) $(3^2 \times 5) + (-5^2 - 9) =$

27) $2[(3^2 \times 5) \times (-6)] =$

28) $(11^2 - 2^2) - (-7^2) =$

29) $(2^2 \times 5) - (64 \div 8) =$

30) $2[(3^2 \times 4) + (35 \div 5)] =$

31) $(4^2 \times 3) \div (-6) =$

32) $3^2[(4^3 \div 16) - (3^3 \div 27)] =$

# Integers and Absolute Value

✎ *Calculate.*

1) $4 - |6 - 10| =$

2) $|14| - \frac{|-18|}{3} =$

3) $\frac{|8 \times -8|}{4} \times \frac{|-20|}{5} =$

4) $|12 \times 3| + \frac{|-81|}{9} =$

5) $4 - |11 - 18| - |3| =$

6) $|18| - \frac{|-12|}{4} =$

7) $\frac{|5 \times -8|}{10} \times \frac{|-22|}{11} =$

8) $|9 \times 3| + \frac{|-36|}{4} =$

9) $|-42 + 7| \times \frac{|-2 \times 5|}{10} =$

10) $6 - |17 - 11| - |5| =$

11) $|13| - \frac{|-54|}{6} =$

12) $\frac{|9 \times -4|}{12} \times \frac{|-45|}{9} =$

13) $|-75 + 50| \times \frac{|-4 \times 5|}{5} =$

14) $\frac{|-26|}{13} \times \frac{|-32|}{8} =$

15) $14 - |8 - 18| - |-12| =$

16) $|29| - \frac{|-20|}{5} =$

17) $\frac{|3 \times 8|}{2} \times \frac{|-33|}{3} =$

18) $|-45 + 15| \times \frac{|-12 \times 5|}{6} =$

19) $\frac{|-50|}{5} \times \frac{|-77|}{11} =$

20) $12 - |2 - 7| - |15| =$

21) $|18| - \frac{|-45|}{15} =$

22) $\frac{|7 \times 8|}{4} \times \frac{|-48|}{12} =$

23) $\frac{|30 \times 2|}{3} \times |-12| =$

24) $\frac{|-36|}{9} \times \frac{|-80|}{8} =$

25) $|-30 + 9| \times \frac{|-8 \times 5|}{8} =$

26) $|16| - \frac{|-18|}{3} =$

27) $12 - |10 - 24| + |5| =$

28) $|-38 + 8| \times \frac{|-5 \times 6|}{10} =$

**Effortless Math Education**

## Answers – Chapter 3

### Adding and Subtracting Integers

| | | | |
|---|---|---|---|
| 1) 6 | 9) 24 | 17) −20 | 25) −13 |
| 2) 35 | 10) −12 | 18) 44 | 26) −17 |
| 3) −16 | 11) −12 | 19) −18 | 27) 3 |
| 4) −9 | 12) 13 | 20) 22 | 28) −37 |
| 5) −4 | 13) 18 | 21) 11 | 29) −15 |
| 6) −11 | 14) −12 | 22) −24 | 30) −29 |
| 7) −4 | 15) −11 | 23) 45 | 31) −12 |
| 8) −15 | 16) −25 | 24) −7 | 32) 33 |

### Multiplying and Dividing Integers

| | | | |
|---|---|---|---|
| 1) 42 | 9) −20 | 17) −14 | 25) 42 |
| 2) −40 | 10) 80 | 18) −28 | 26) 81 |
| 3) −6 | 11) −4 | 19) −25 | 27) −7 |
| 4) −8 | 12) −3 | 20) −11 | 28) 120 |
| 5) −24 | 13) −35 | 21) 90 | 29) −66 |
| 6) 99 | 14) 120 | 22) −27 | 30) 60 |
| 7) −2 | 15) −2 | 23) −2 | 31) −8 |
| 8) −12 | 16) −2 | 24) −12 | 32) −5 |

## Order of Operation

| | | | |
|---|---|---|---|
| 1) 22 | 9) 39 | 17) −24 | 25) −37 |
| 2) −9 | 10) −63 | 18) −40 | 26) 11 |
| 3) 33 | 11) −18 | 19) 38 | 27) −540 |
| 4) −48 | 12) 70 | 20) −42 | 28) 166 |
| 5) 66 | 13) 30 | 21) −8 | 29) 12 |
| 6) 4 | 14) −81 | 22) −72 | 30) 86 |
| 7) 22 | 15) 33 | 23) 63 | 31) −8 |
| 8) 15 | 16) −24 | 24) −59 | 32) 27 |

## Integers and Absolute Value

| | | | |
|---|---|---|---|
| 1) 0 | 8) 36 | 15) −8 | 22) 56 |
| 2) 8 | 9) 35 | 16) 25 | 23) 240 |
| 3) 64 | 10) −5 | 17) 132 | 24) 40 |
| 4) 45 | 11) 4 | 18) 300 | 25) 105 |
| 5) −6 | 12) 15 | 19) 70 | 26) 10 |
| 6) 15 | 13) 100 | 20) −8 | 27) 3 |
| 7) 8 | 14) 8 | 21) 15 | 28) 90 |

# Chapter 4: Ratios and Proportions

**Math Topics that you'll learn in this Chapter:**

- ✓ Simplifying Ratios
- ✓ Proportional Ratios
- ✓ Similarity and Ratios
- ✓ Simple Interest

29

## Simplifying Ratios

✎ *Simplify each ratio.*

1) $3:21 =$ ___ : ___

2) $4:16 =$ ___ : ___

3) $\frac{2}{28} = -$

4) $\frac{18}{45} = -$

5) $10:30 =$ ___ : ___

6) $5:30 =$ ___ : ___

7) $\frac{34}{38} = -$

8) $\frac{45}{63} = -$

9) $10:45 =$ ___ : ___

10) $20:30 =$ ___ : ___

11) $\frac{40}{64} = -$

12) $\frac{10}{110} = -$

13) $8:12 =$ ___ : ___

14) $16:20 =$ ___ : ___

15) $\frac{24}{48} = -$

16) $\frac{21}{77} = -$

17) $8:24 =$ ___ : ___

18) $9 \text{ to } 36 =$ ___ : ___

19) $\frac{64}{72} = -$

20) $\frac{45}{60} = -$

21) $12:15 =$ ___ : ___

22) $18:54 =$ ___ : ___

23) $\frac{36}{54} = -$

24) $\frac{48}{104} = -$

25) $12:48 =$ ___ : ___

26) $18:72 =$ ___ : ___

27) $\frac{15}{75} = -$

28) $\frac{46}{52} = -$

## Proportional Ratios

✎ *Solve each proportion for $x$.*

1) $\frac{4}{7} = \frac{8}{x}$, $x = $ _____

2) $\frac{9}{12} = \frac{x}{8}$, $x = $ _____

3) $\frac{3}{5} = \frac{12}{x}$, $x = $ _____

4) $\frac{3}{10} = \frac{x}{50}$, $x = $ _____

5) $\frac{3}{11} = \frac{15}{x}$, $x = $ _____

6) $\frac{6}{15} = \frac{x}{45}$, $x = $ _____

7) $\frac{6}{19} = \frac{12}{x}$, $x = $ _____

8) $\frac{7}{16} = \frac{x}{32}$, $x = $ _____

9) $\frac{18}{21} = \frac{54}{x}$, $x = $ _____

10) $\frac{13}{15} = \frac{39}{x}$, $x = $ _____

11) $\frac{9}{13} = \frac{72}{x}$, $x = $ _____

12) $\frac{8}{30} = \frac{x}{180}$, $x = $ _____

13) $\frac{3}{19} = \frac{9}{x}$, $x = $ _____

14) $\frac{1}{3} = \frac{x}{90}$, $x = $ _____

15) $\frac{25}{45} = \frac{x}{9}$, $x = $ _____

16) $\frac{1}{6} = \frac{9}{x}$, $x = $ _____

17) $\frac{7}{9} = \frac{63}{x}$, $x = $ _____

18) $\frac{54}{72} = \frac{x}{8}$, $x = $ _____

19) $\frac{32}{40} = \frac{4}{x}$, $x = $ _____

20) $\frac{21}{42} = \frac{x}{6}$, $x = $ _____

21) $\frac{56}{72} = \frac{7}{x}$, $x = $ _____

22) $\frac{1}{14} = \frac{x}{42}$, $x = $ _____

23) $\frac{5}{7} = \frac{75}{x}$, $x = $ _____

24) $\frac{30}{48} = \frac{x}{8}$, $x = $ _____

25) $\frac{36}{88} = \frac{9}{x}$, $x = $ _____

26) $\frac{62}{68} = \frac{x}{34}$, $x = $ _____

27) $\frac{42}{60} = \frac{x}{10}$, $x = $ _____

28) $\frac{8}{9} = \frac{x}{108}$, $x = $ _____

29) $\frac{40}{6} = \frac{x}{3}$, $x = $ _____

30) $\frac{88}{121} = \frac{x}{11}$, $x = $ _____

31) $\frac{10}{24} = \frac{x}{48}$, $x = $ _____

32) $\frac{32}{80} = \frac{x}{10}$, $x = $ _____

## Create Proportion

✍ *State if each pair of ratios form a proportion.*

1) $\frac{3}{8}$ and $\frac{24}{50}$

2) $\frac{3}{11}$ and $\frac{6}{22}$

3) $\frac{4}{5}$ and $\frac{16}{20}$

4) $\frac{5}{11}$ and $\frac{12}{33}$

5) $\frac{5}{10}$ and $\frac{15}{30}$

6) $\frac{4}{13}$ and $\frac{8}{24}$

7) $\frac{6}{9}$ and $\frac{24}{36}$

8) $\frac{7}{12}$ and $\frac{14}{20}$

9) $\frac{3}{8}$ and $\frac{27}{72}$

10) $\frac{12}{20}$ and $\frac{36}{60}$

11) $\frac{11}{12}$ and $\frac{55}{60}$

12) $\frac{12}{15}$ and $\frac{24}{25}$

13) $\frac{15}{19}$ and $\frac{20}{38}$

14) $\frac{10}{14}$ and $\frac{40}{56}$

15) $\frac{11}{13}$ and $\frac{44}{39}$

16) $\frac{15}{16}$ and $\frac{30}{32}$

17) $\frac{17}{19}$ and $\frac{34}{48}$

18) $\frac{5}{18}$ and $\frac{15}{54}$

19) $\frac{3}{14}$ and $\frac{18}{42}$

20) $\frac{7}{11}$ and $\frac{14}{32}$

21) $\frac{8}{11}$ and $\frac{32}{44}$

22) $\frac{8}{14}$ and $\frac{24}{54}$

✍ *Solve.*

23) The ratio of boys to girls in a class is 3 : 4. If there are 27 boys in the class, how many girls are in that class? _____

24) The ratio of red marbles to blue marbles in a bag is 5 : 6. If there are 66 marbles in the bag, how many of the marbles are red? _____

25) You can buy 6 cans of green beans at a supermarket for $3.60. How much does it cost to buy 48 cans of green beans? _____

# Similarity and Ratios

✎ *Each pair of figures is similar. Find the missing side.*

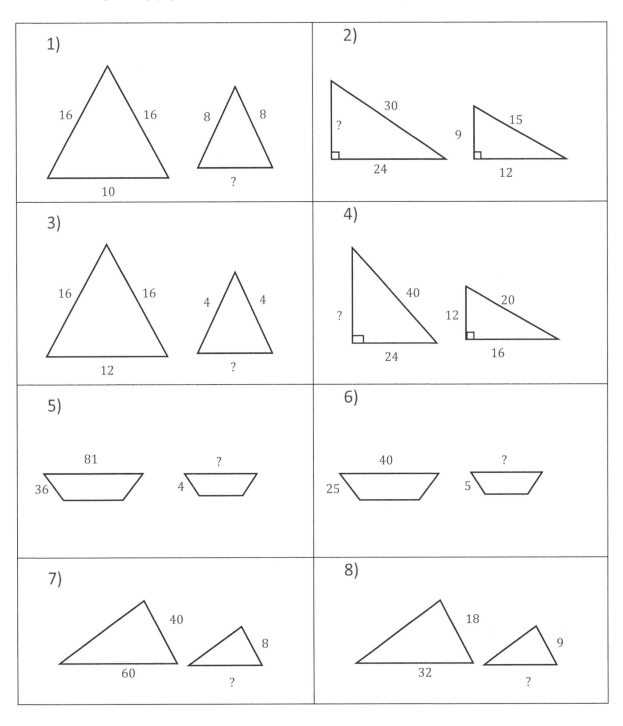

# Simple Interest

✎ *Determine the simple interest for these loans.*

1) $400 at 6% for 4 years. $___

2) $580 at 3.5% for 5 years. $__

3) $320 at 4% for 6 years. $___

4) $510 at 8% for 3 years. $___

5) $690 at 5% for 6 months. $___

6) $620 at 7% for 3 years. $___

7) $650 at 4.5% for 10 years. $___

8) $850 at 4% for 2 years. $___

9) $640 at 7% for 3 years. $___

10) $300 at 9% for 9 months. $___

11) $760 at 8% for 2 years. $__

12) $910 at 5% for 5 years. $___

13) $540 at 3% for 6 years. $___

14) $780 at 2.5% for 4 years. $___

15) $1,600 at 7% for 3 months. $___

16) $310 at 4% for 4 years. $___

17) $950 at 6% for 5 years. $___

18) $280 at 8% for 7 years. $___

19) $310 at 6% for 3 years. $___

20) $990 at 5% for 4 months. $___

21) $380 at 6% for 5 years. $___

22) $580 at 6% for 4 years. $___

23) $1,200 at 4% for 5 years. $___

24) $3,100 at 5% for 6 years. $___

25) $5,200 at 8% for 2 years. $___

26) $1,400 at 4% for 3 years. $___

27) $300 at 3% for 8 months. $___

28) $150 at 3.5% for 4 years. $___

29) $170 at 6% for 2 years. $___

30) $940 at 8% for 5 years. $___

31) $960 at 1.5% for 8 years. $__

32) $240 at 5% for 4 months. $___

33) $280 at 2% for 5 years. $___

34) $880 at 3% for 2 years. $___

35) $2,200 at 4.5% for 2 years. $___

36) $2,400 at 7% for 3 years. $___

37) $1,800 at 5% for 6 months. $___

38) $190 at 4% for 2 years. $___

39) $480 at 6% for 5 years. $___

40) $700 at 5% for 6 years. $__

**Effortless Math Education**

## Answers – Chapter 4

### Simplifying Ratios

1) $1:7$

2) $1:4$

3) $\frac{1}{14}$

4) $\frac{2}{5}$

5) $1:3$

6) $1:6$

7) $\frac{17}{19}$

8) $\frac{5}{7}$

9) $2:9$

10) $2:3$

11) $\frac{5}{8}$

12) $\frac{1}{11}$

13) $2:3$

14) $4:5$

15) $\frac{1}{2}$

16) $\frac{3}{11}$

17) $1:3$

18) $1$ to $4$

19) $\frac{8}{9}$

20) $\frac{3}{4}$

21) $4:5$

22) $1:3$

23) $\frac{2}{3}$

24) $\frac{6}{13}$

25) $1:4$

26) $1:4$

27) $\frac{1}{5}$

28) $\frac{23}{26}$

### Proportional Ratios

1) $x = 14$

2) $x = 6$

3) $x = 20$

4) $x = 15$

5) $x = 55$

6) $x = 18$

7) $x = 38$

8) $x = 14$

9) $x = 63$

10) $x = 45$

11) $x = 104$

12) $x = 48$

13) $x = 57$

14) $x = 30$

15) $x = 5$

16) $x = 54$

17) $x = 81$

18) $x = 6$

19) $x = 5$

20) $x = 3$

21) $x = 9$

22) $x = 3$

23) $x = 105$

24) $x = 5$

25) $x = 22$

26) $x = 31$

27) $x = 7$

28) $x = 96$

29) $x = 20$

30) $x = 8$

31) $x = 20$

32) $x = 4$

## Create Proportion

1) *No*

2) *Yes*

3) *Yes*

4) *No*

5) *Yes*

6) *No*

7) *Yes*

8) *No*

9) *Yes*

10) *Yes*

11) *Yes*

12) *No*

13) *No*

14) *Yes*

15) *No*

16) *Yes*

17) *No*

18) *Yes*

19) *No*

20) *No*

21) *Yes*

22) *No*

23) 36 *girls*

24) 30 *red marbles*

25) $28.80

## Similarity and Ratios

1) 5

2) 18

3) 3

4) 32

5) 9

6) 8

7) 12

8) 16

## Simple Interest

1) $96

2) $101.50

3) $76.80

4) $122.40

5) $17.25

6) $130.20

7) $292.50

8) $68

9) $134.40

10) $20.25

11) $121.60

12) $227.50

13) $97.20

14) $78

15) $28

16) $49.60

17) $285

18) $156.80

19) $55.80

20) $16.5

21) $114

22) $139.20

23) $240

24) $930

25) $832

26) $168

27) $6

28) $21

29) $20.40

30) $376

31) $115.20

32) $4

33) $28

34) $52.80

35) $198

36) $504

37) $45

38) $15.20

39) $144

40) $210

# Chapter 5:
# Percentage

**Math Topics that you'll learn in this Chapter:**

- ✓ Percent Problems
- ✓ Percent of Increase and Decrease
- ✓ Discount, Tax and Tip

39

## Percent Problems

✍ *Solve each problem.*

1) What is 4 percent of 280? _____

2) What is 25 percent of 500? _____

3) What is 10 percent of 460? _____

4) What is 34 percent of 260? _____

5) What is 60 percent of 850? _____

6) 63 is what percent of 300? _____%

7) 80 is what percent of 400? _____%

8) 70 is what percent of 700? _____%

9) 84 is what percent of 600? ___%

10) 90 is what percent of 300? ___%

11) 24 is what percent of 150? ___%

12) 12 is what percent of 80? _____%

13) 4 is what percent of 50? _____%

14) 110 is what percent of 500? _%

15) 16 is what percent of 400? __%

16) 39 is what percent of 300? ___%

17) 56 is what percent of 200? ___%

18) 30 is what percent of 500? ___%

19) 84 is what percent of 700? ___%

20) 40 is what percent of 500? __%

21) 26 is what percent of 100? __ %

22) 45 is what percent of 900? __%

23) 60 is what percent of 400? ___%

24) 18 is what percent of 900? ___%

25) 75 is what percent of 250? ___%

26) 27 is what percent of 900? ___%

27) 49 is what percent of 700? ___%

28) 81 is what percent of 900? ___%

29) 90 is what percent of 500? ___%

30) 82 is what percent of 410? ___%

31) 14 is 35 percent of what number? _____

32) 90 is 6 percent of what number? _____

33) 80 is 40 percent of what number? _____

34) 80 is 20 percent of what number? _____

35) 30 is 6 percent of what number? _____

36) 64 is 8 percent of what number? _____

# Percent of Increase and Decrease

✑ *Solve each percent of change word problem.*

1) Bob got a raise, and his hourly wage increased from $30 to $42. What is the percent increase? _____ %

2) The price of gasoline rose from $4.40 to $4.62 in one month. By what percent did the gas price rise? _____ %

3) In a class, the number of students has been increased from 25 to 32. What is the percent increase? _____ %

4) The price of a pair of shoes increases from $24 to $30. What is the percent increase? ____ %

5) In a class, the number of students has been decreased from 24 to 18. What is the percentage decrease? _____ %

6) Nick got a raise, and his hourly wage increased from $50 to $55. What is the percent increase? _____ %

7) A coat was originally priced at $60. It went on sale for $54. What was the percent that the coat was discounted? _____ %

8) The price of a pair of shoes increases from $12 to $18. What is the percent increase? ____ %

9) A house was purchased in 2002 for $150,000. It is now valued at $132,000. What is the rate (percent) of depreciation for the house?____ %

10) The price of gasoline rose from $4.00 to $4.20 in one month. By what percent did the gas price rise? _____ %

# Discount, Tax and Tip

✍ *Find the missing values.*

1) Original price of a computer: $540, Tax: 6%, Selling price: $_____

2) Original price of a sofa: $400, Tax: 14%, Selling price: $_____

3) Original price of a table: $560, Tax: 15%, Selling price: $_____

4) Original price of a cell phone: $740, Tax: 24%, Selling price: $_____

5) Original price of a printer: $400, Tax: 22%, Selling price: $_____

6) Original price of a computer: $600, Tax: 15%, Selling price: $_____

7) Restaurant bill: $24.00, Tip: 25%, Final amount: $_____

8) Original price of a cell phone: $300 Tax: 8%, Selling price: $_____

9) Original price of a carpet: $800, Tax: 25%, Selling price: $_____

10) Original price of a camera: $200 Discount: 35%, Selling price: $_____

11) Original price of a dress: $560 Discount: 10%, Selling price: $____

12) Original price of a monitor: $420 Discount: 6%, Selling price: $____

13) Original price of a laptop: $880 Discount: 16%, Selling price: $____

14) Restaurant bill: $64.00, Tip: 20%, Final amount: $____

# Answers – Chapter 5

**Percent Problems**

| | | |
|---|---|---|
| 1) 11.2 | 13) 8% | 25) 30% |
| 2) 125 | 14) 22% | 26) 3% |
| 3) 46 | 15) 4% | 27) 7% |
| 4) 88.4 | 16) 13% | 28) 9% |
| 5) 510 | 17) 28% | 29) 18% |
| 6) 21% | 18) 6% | 30) 20% |
| 7) 20% | 19) 12% | 31) 40 |
| 8) 10% | 20) 8% | 32) 1,500 |
| 9) 14% | 21) 26% | 33) 200 |
| 10) 30% | 22) 5% | 34) 400 |
| 11) 16% | 23) 15% | 35) 500 |
| 12) 15% | 24) 2% | 36) 800 |

**Percent of Increase and Decrease**

| | | |
|---|---|---|
| 1) 40% | 5) 25% | 9) 12% |
| 2) 5% | 6) 10% | 10) 5% |
| 3) 28% | 7) 10% | |
| 4) 25% | 8) 50% | |

**Effortless Math Education**

## Discount, Tax and Tip

1) $572.40

2) $456

3) $644

4) $917.60

5) $488

6) $690

7) $30.00

8) $324

9) $1,000

10) $130

11) $504

12) $394.8

13) $739.2

14) $76.80

# Chapter 6:
# Expressions and
# Variables

**Math Topics that you'll learn in this Chapter:**

- ✓ Simplifying Variable Expressions
- ✓ Simplifying Polynomial Expressions
- ✓ Evaluating One Variable
- ✓ Evaluating Two Variables
- ✓ The Distributive Property

## Simplifying Variable Expressions

✎ *Simplify and write the answer.*

1) $6x + 2 + 3x =$

2) $7x + 4 - 6x =$

3) $-1 - x^2 - 9x^2 =$

4) $(-5)(6x - 2) =$

5) $3 + 10x^2 + 2x =$

6) $8x^2 + 6x + 7x^2 =$

7) $2x^2 - 5x - 7x =$

8) $x - 3 + 5 - 3x =$

9) $2 - 3x + 12 - 2x =$

10) $5x^2 - 12x^2 + 8x =$

11) $2x^2 + 6x + 3x^2 =$

12) $2x^2 - 2x - x =$

13) $2x^2 - (-8x + 6) =$

14) $4x + 6(2 - 5x) =$

15) $10x + 8(10x - 6) =$

16) $9(-2x - 6) - 5 =$

17) $32x - 4 + 23 + 2x =$

18) $8x - 12x - x^2 + 13 =$

19) $(-6)(8x - 4) + 10x =$

20) $14x - 5(5 - 8x) =$

21) $23x + 4(9x + 3) + 12 =$

22) $3(-7x + 5) + 20x =$

23) $12x - 3x(x + 9) =$

24) $7x + 5x(3 - 3x) =$

25) $5x(-8x + 12) + 14x =$

26) $40x + 12 + 2x^2 =$

27) $5x(x - 3) - 10 =$

28) $8x - 7 + 8x + 2x^2 =$

29) $6x - 2x^2 - 6x^2 - 5 =$

30) $3 + x^2 - 4x^2 - 10x =$

31) $10x + 6x^2 + 5x + 18 =$

32) $20 + 12x^2 + 7x - 6x^2 =$

## Simplifying Polynomial Expressions

✍ *Simplify and write the answer.*

1) $(3x^3 + 4x^2) - (10x + 3x^2) = $ _____

2) $(-4x^5 + 4x^3) - (6x^3 + 5x^2) = $ _____

3) $(10x^4 + 6x^2) - (x^2 - 8x^4) = $ _____

4) $6x - 2x^2 - 3(2x^2 + 5x^3) = $ _____

5) $(2x^3 - 3) + 3(2x^2 - 3x^3) = $ _____

6) $4(4x^3 - 2x) - (3x^3 - 2x^4) = $ _____

7) $2(4x - 3x^3) - 3(3x^3 + 4x^2) = $ _____

8) $(2x^2 - 2x) - (2x^3 + 5x^2) = $ _____

9) $2x^3 - (4x^4 + 2x) + x^2 = $ _____

10) $x^4 - 9(x^2 + x) - 5x = $ _____

11) $(-2x^2 - x^4) + (4x^4 - x^2) = $ _____

12) $4x^2 - 5x^3 + 15x^4 - 12x^3 = $ _____

13) $3x^2 - 2x^4 + 12x^4 - 10x^3 = $ _____

14) $4x^2 + 6x^3 - 8x^2 + 14x = $ _____

15) $3x^4 - 6x^5 + 7x^4 - 9x^2 = $ _____

16) $5x^3 + 15x - 4x^2 - 3x^3 = $ _____

## Evaluating One Variable

✍ *Evaluate each expression using the value given.*

1) $x = 2 \Rightarrow 5x - 10 =$

2) $x = 3 \Rightarrow 6x - 12 =$

3) $x = 4 \Rightarrow 6x + 8 =$

4) $x = 6 \Rightarrow 2x + 4 =$

5) $x = 4 \Rightarrow 4x - 8 =$

6) $x = 2 \Rightarrow 5x - 2x + 10 =$

7) $x = 3 \Rightarrow 2x - x - 6 =$

8) $x = 4 \Rightarrow 6x - 3x + 4 =$

9) $x = -2 \Rightarrow 4x - 6x - 5 =$

10) $x = -1 \Rightarrow 3x - 5x + 11 =$

11) $x = 1 \Rightarrow x - 7x + 12 =$

12) $x = 2 \Rightarrow 2(-3x + 4) =$

13) $x = 3 \Rightarrow 4(-5x - 2) =$

14) $x = 2 \Rightarrow 5(-2x - 4) =$

15) $x = -2 \Rightarrow 3(-4x - 5) =$

16) $x = 3 \Rightarrow 8x + 5 =$

17) $x = -3 \Rightarrow 12x + 9 =$

18) $x = -1 \Rightarrow 9x - 8 =$

19) $x = 2 \Rightarrow 16x - 10 =$

20) $x = 1 \Rightarrow 4x + 3 =$

21) $x = 5 \Rightarrow 7x - 2 =$

22) $x = 7 \Rightarrow 28 - x =$

23) $x = 8 \Rightarrow 4x - 12 =$

24) $x = 10 \Rightarrow 44 - 3x =$

25) $x = 4 \Rightarrow 10x - 6 =$

26) $x = 7 \Rightarrow 6x - x + 9 =$

# Evaluating Two Variables

✏ *Evaluate each expression using the values given.*

1) $x + 4y, x = 3, y = 2$ _____

2) $6x + 3y, x = -2, y = -3$ _____

3) $x + 5y, x = 2, y = -1$ _____

4) $3a - (10 - b), a = 3, b = 4$ _____

5) $4a - (6 - 3b), a = 1, b = 4$ _____

6) $a - (8 - 2b), a = 2, b = 5$ _____

7) $3z + 21 + 5k, z = 4, k = 1$ _____

8) $-7a + 4b, a = 6, b = 3$ _____

9) $-4a + 3b, a = 2, b = 4$ _____

10) $-6a + 6b, a = 4, b = 3$ _____

11) $-8a + 2b, a = 4, b = 6$ _____

12) $4x + 6y, x = 6, y = 3$ _____

13) $2x + 9y, x = 8, y = 1$ _____

14) $x - 7y, x = 9, y = 4$ _____

15) $5x - 4y, x = 6, y = 3$ _____

16) $2z + 14 + 8k, z = 4, k = 1$ _____

17) $6x + 3y, x = 3, y = 8$ _____

18) $5a - 6b, a = -3, b = -1$ _____

19) $6a + 2b, a = -6, b = 4$ _____

20) $-3a - b, a = 5, b = -6$ _____

21) $-6a + 2b, a = 6, b = -3$ _____

22) $-6a + 8b, a = 6, b = -1$ _____

# The Distributive Property

✎ *Use the distributive property to simply each expression.*

1) $(-2)(10x + 3) =$

2) $(-3x + 5)(-5) =$

3) $11(-3x + 3) =$

4) $6(5 - 4x) =$

5) $(6 - 5x)(-4) =$

6) $9(8 - 2x) =$

7) $(-4x + 6)5 =$

8) $(-2x + 7)(-8) =$

9) $8(-4x + 7) =$

10) $(-9x + 5)(-3) =$

11) $8(-x + 9) =$

12) $7(2 - 6x) =$

13) $(-12x + 4)(-3) =$

14) $(-6)(-10x + 6) =$

15) $(-5)(5 - 11x) =$

16) $9(4 - 8x) =$

17) $(-6x + 2)7 =$

18) $(-9)(1 - 12x) =$

19) $(-3)(4 - 6x) =$

20) $(2 - 8x)(-2) =$

21) $20(2 - x) =$

22) $12(-4x + 3) =$

23) $12(3 - 4x) =$

24) $(-6x + 6)3 =$

25) $(-10x + 6)(-3) =$

26) $13(4 - 7x) =$

**Effortless Math Education**

# Answers – Chapter 6

## Simplifying Variable Expressions

1) $9x + 2$

2) $x + 4$

3) $-10x^2 - 1$

4) $-30x + 10$

5) $10x^2 + 2x + 3$

6) $15x^2 + 6x$

7) $2x^2 - 12x$

8) $-2x + 2$

9) $-5x + 14$

10) $-7x^2 + 8x$

11) $5x^2 + 6x$

12) $2x^2 - 3x$

13) $2x^2 + 8x - 6$

14) $-26x + 12$

15) $90x - 48$

16) $-18x - 59$

17) $34x + 19$

18) $-x^2 - 4x + 13$

19) $-38x + 24$

20) $54x - 25$

21) $59x + 24$

22) $-x + 15$

23) $-3x^2 - 15x$

24) $-15x^2 + 22x$

25) $-40x^2 + 74x$

26) $2x^2 + 40x + 12$

27) $5x^2 - 15x - 10$

28) $2x^2 + 16x - 7$

29) $-8x^2 + 6x - 5$

30) $-3x^2 - 10x + 3$

31) $6x^2 + 15x + 18$

32) $6x^2 + 7x + 20$

## Simplifying Polynomial Expressions

1) $3x^3 + x^2 - 10x$

2) $-4x^5 - 2x^3 - 5x^2$

3) $18x^4 + 5x^2$

4) $-15x^3 - 8x^2 + 6x$

5) $-7x^3 + 6x^2 - 3$

6) $2x^4 + 13x^3 - 8x$

7) $-15x^3 - 12x^2 + 8x$

8) $-2x^3 - 3x^2 - 2x$

9) $-4x^4 + 2x^3 + x^2 - 2x$

10) $x^4 - 9x^2 - 14x$

11) $3x^4 - 3x^2$

12) $15x^4 - 17x^3 + 4x^2$

13) $10x^4 - 10x^3 + 3x^2$

14) $6x^3 - 4x^2 + 14x$

15) $-6x^5 + 10x^4 - 9x^2$

16) $2x^3 - 4x^2 + 15x$

## Evaluating One Variable

1) 0

2) 6

3) 32

4) 16

5) 8

6) 16

7) −3

8) 16

9) −1

10) 13

11) 6

12) −4

13) −68

14) −40

15) 9

16) 29

17) −27

18) −17

19) 22

20) 7

21) 33

22) 21

23) 20

24) 14

25) 34

26) 44

## Evaluating Two Variables

1) 11
2) −21
3) −3
4) 3
5) 10
6) 4

7) 38
8) −30
9) 4
10) −6
11) −20
12) 42

13) 25
14) −19
15) 18
16) 30
17) 42
18) −9

19) −28
20) −9
21) −42
22) −44

## The Distributive Property

1) $-20x - 6$
2) $15x - 25$
3) $-33x + 33$
4) $-24x + 30$
5) $20x - 24$
6) $-18x + 72$
7) $-20x + 30$
8) $16x - 56$
9) $-32x + 56$

10) $27x - 15$
11) $-8x + 72$
12) $-42x + 14$
13) $36x - 12$
14) $60x - 36$
15) $55x - 25$
16) $-72x + 36$
17) $-42x + 14$
18) $108x - 9$

19) $18x - 12$
20) $16x - 4$
21) $-20x + 40$
22) $-48x + 36$
23) $-48x + 36$
24) $-18x + 18$
25) $30x - 18$
26) $-91x + 52$

# Chapter 7: Equations and Inequalities

**Math Topics that you'll learn in this Chapter:**

- ✓ One–Step Equations
- ✓ Multi–Step Equations
- ✓ System of Equations
- ✓ Graphing Single–Variable Inequalities
- ✓ One–Step Inequalities
- ✓ Multi–Step Inequalities

## One–Step Equations

🖎 *Solve each equation for x.*

1) $x - 18 = 28 \Rightarrow x =$ _____

2) $19 = -5 + x \Rightarrow x =$ _____

3) $15 - x = 6 \Rightarrow x =$ _____

4) $x - 24 = 29 \Rightarrow x =$ _____

5) $24 - x = 17 \Rightarrow x =$ _____

6) $16 - x = 3 \Rightarrow x =$ _____

7) $x + 14 = 12 \Rightarrow x =$ _____

8) $26 + x = 8 \Rightarrow x =$ _____

9) $x + 9 = -18 \Rightarrow x =$ _____

10) $x + 21 = 11 \Rightarrow x =$ _____

11) $17 = -5 + x \Rightarrow x =$ _____

12) $x + 20 = 29 \Rightarrow x =$ _____

13) $x - 13 = 19 \Rightarrow x =$ _____

14) $x + 9 = -17 \Rightarrow x =$ _____

15) $x + 4 = -23 \Rightarrow x =$ _____

16) $16 = -9 + x \Rightarrow x =$ _____

17) $4x = 28 \Rightarrow x =$ _____

18) $21 = -7x \Rightarrow x =$ _____

19) $12x = -12 \Rightarrow x =$ _____

20) $13x = 39 \Rightarrow x =$ _____

21) $8x = -16 \Rightarrow x =$ _____

22) $\frac{x}{2} = -5 \Rightarrow x =$ _____

23) $\frac{x}{9} = 6 \Rightarrow x =$ _____

24) $27 = \frac{x}{5} \Rightarrow x =$ _____

25) $\frac{x}{4} = -3 \Rightarrow x =$ _____

26) $x \div 8 = 7 \Rightarrow x =$ _____

27) $x \div 2 = -3 \Rightarrow x =$ _____

28) $8x = 56 \Rightarrow x =$ _____

29) $9x = 54 \Rightarrow x =$ _____

30) $7x = -35 \Rightarrow x =$ _____

31) $60 = -10x \Rightarrow x =$ _____

# Multi –Step Equations

✎ *Solve each equation.*

1) $4x - 7 = 13 \Rightarrow x = $ ___

2) $26 = -(x - 4) \Rightarrow x = $ ___

3) $-(5 - x) = 19 \Rightarrow x = $ ___

4) $35 = -x + 14 \Rightarrow x = $ ___

5) $2(3 - 2x) = 10 \Rightarrow x = $ ___

6) $3x - 3 = 15 \Rightarrow x = $ ___

7) $32 = -x + 15 \Rightarrow x = $ ___

8) $-(10 - x) = -13 \Rightarrow x = $ ___

9) $-4(7 + x) = 4 \Rightarrow x = $ ___

10) $22 = 2x - 8 \Rightarrow x = $ ___

11) $-6(3 + x) = 6 \Rightarrow x = $ ___

12) $-3 = 3x - 15 \Rightarrow x = $ ___

13) $-7(12 + x) = 7 \Rightarrow x = $ ___

14) $8(6 - 4x) = 16 \Rightarrow x = $ ___

15) $18 - 4x = -9 - x \Rightarrow x = $ ___

16) $6(4 - x) = 30 \Rightarrow x = $ ___

17) $15 - 3x = -5 - x \Rightarrow x = $ ___

18) $9(-7 - 3x) = 18 \Rightarrow x = $ ___

19) $16 - 2x = -4 - 7x \Rightarrow x = $ ___

20) $14 - 2x = 14 + x \Rightarrow x = $ ___

21) $21 - 3x = -7 - 10x \Rightarrow x = $ __

22) $8 - 2x = 11 + x \Rightarrow x = $ ___

23) $10 + 12x = -8 + 6x \Rightarrow x = $ __

24) $25 + 20x = -5 + 5x \Rightarrow x = $ __

25) $16 - x = -8 - 7x \Rightarrow x = $ ___

26) $17 - 3x = 13 + x \Rightarrow x = $ ___

27) $22 + 5x = -8 - x \Rightarrow x = $ ___

28) $-9(7 + x) = 9 \Rightarrow x = $ ___

29) $12 + 2x = -4 - 2x \Rightarrow x = $ ___

30) $12 - x = 2 - 3x \Rightarrow x = $ ___

31) $19 - x = -1 - 11x \Rightarrow x = $ ___

32) $14 - 3x = -5 - 4x \Rightarrow x = $ ___

# System of Equations

✎ *Solve each system of equations.*

1) $2x + 3y = 15$     $x =$

   $x - 3y = 3$    $y =$

2) $y = x + 3$    $x =$

   $x + y = -5$    $y =$

3) $x + 3y = 6$    $x =$

   $2x + 8y = -12$    $y =$

4) $2x + y = 5$    $x =$

   $-3x + 6y = 0$    $y =$

5) $10x - 8y = -15$    $x =$

   $-6x + 4y = 13$    $y =$

6) $-3x - 4y = 5$    $x =$

   $x - 2y = 5$    $y =$

7) $5x - 12y = -19$    $x =$

   $-6x + 7y = 8$    $y =$

8) $5x - 7y = -2$    $x =$

   $-x - 2y = -3$    $y =$

9) $-x + 3y = 3$    $x =$

   $-7x + 8y = -5$    $y =$

10) $-4x + 3y = -18$    $x =$

   $4x - y = 14$    $y =$

11) $6x - 7y = -8$    $x =$

   $-x - 4y = -9$    $y =$

12) $-3x + 2y = -16$    $x =$

   $4x - y = 13$    $y =$

13) $2x + 3y = 8$    $x =$

   $-3x + 2y = 1$    $y =$

14) $y = -x + 3$    $x =$

   $3y + 5x = -1$    $y =$

15) $2x + 3y = 12$    $x =$

   $x + y = 5$    $y =$

16) $y = x - 1$    $x =$

   $y = 2x + 2$    $y =$

# Graphing Single–Variable Inequalities

🖎 *Graph each inequality.*

1) $x < 5$

2) $x \geq 2$

3) $x \geq -4$

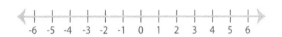

4) $x \leq -1$

5) $x > -1$

6) $3 > x$

7) $2 \leq x$

8) $x > 0$

9) $-3 \leq x$

10) $-4 \leq x$

11) $x \leq 6$

12) $1 \leq x$

13) $-4 < x$

14) $x > -5$

## One–Step Inequalities

✎ *Solve each inequality for x.*

1) $x - 9 < 20 \Rightarrow$ _____

2) $14 \leq -6 + x \Rightarrow$ _____

3) $x - 31 > 9 \Rightarrow$ _____

4) $x + 28 \geq 36 \Rightarrow$ _____

5) $x - 24 > 17 \Rightarrow$ _____

6) $x + 5 \geq 3 \Rightarrow$ _____

7) $x + 14 < 12 \Rightarrow$ _____

8) $26 + x \leq 8 \Rightarrow$ _____

9) $x + 9 \geq -18 \Rightarrow$ _____

10) $x + 24 < 11 \Rightarrow$ _____

11) $17 \leq -5 + x \Rightarrow$ _____

12) $x + 25 > 29 \Rightarrow$ _____

13) $x - 17 \geq 19 \Rightarrow$ _____

14) $x + 8 > -17 \Rightarrow$ _____

15) $x + 8 < -23 \Rightarrow$ _____

16) $16 \leq -5 + x \Rightarrow$ _____

17) $4x \leq 12 \Rightarrow$ _____

18) $28 \geq -7x \Rightarrow$ _____

19) $2x > -14 \Rightarrow$ _____

20) $13x \leq 39 \Rightarrow$ _____

21) $-8x > -16 \Rightarrow$ _____

22) $\frac{x}{2} < -6 \Rightarrow$ _____

23) $\frac{x}{6} > 6 \Rightarrow$ _____

24) $27 \leq \frac{x}{4} \Rightarrow$ _____

25) $\frac{x}{8} < -3 \Rightarrow$ _____

26) $6x \geq 18 \Rightarrow$ _____

27) $5x \geq -25 \Rightarrow$ _____

28) $3x > 45 \Rightarrow$ _____

29) $9x \leq 72 \Rightarrow$ _____

30) $-6x < -36 \Rightarrow$ _____

31) $70 > -10x \Rightarrow$ _____

# Multi –Step Inequalities

✍ *Solve each inequality.*

1) $2x - 6 \leq 4 \rightarrow$ _____

2) $2 + 3x \geq 17 \rightarrow$ _____

3) $9 + 3x \geq 36 \rightarrow$ _____

4) $2x - 6 \leq 18 \rightarrow$ _____

5) $3x - 4 \leq 23 \rightarrow$ _____

6) $7x - 5 \leq 51 \rightarrow$ _____

7) $4x - 9 \leq 27 \rightarrow$ _____

8) $6x - 11 \leq 13 \rightarrow$ _____

9) $5x - 7 \leq 33 \rightarrow$ _____

10) $6 + 2x \geq 28 \rightarrow$ _____

11) $8 + 3x \geq 35 \rightarrow$ _____

12) $4 + 6x < 34 \rightarrow$ _____

13) $3 + 2x \geq 53 \rightarrow$ _____

14) $7 - 6x > 56 + x \rightarrow$ _____

15) $9 + 4x \geq 39 + 2x \rightarrow$ _____

16) $3 + 5x \geq 43 \rightarrow$ _____

17) $4 - 7x < 60 \rightarrow$ _____

18) $11 - 4x \geq 55 \rightarrow$ _____

19) $12 + x \geq 48 - 2x \rightarrow$ _____

20) $10 - 10x \leq -20 \rightarrow$ _____

21) $5 - 9x \geq -40 \rightarrow$ _____

22) $8 - 7x \geq 36 \rightarrow$ _____

23) $6 + 10x < 69 + 3x \rightarrow$ _____

24) $5 + 4x < 26 - 3x \rightarrow$ _____

25) $10 + 11x < 59 + 4x \rightarrow$ ____

26) $3 + 9x \geq 48 - 6x \rightarrow$ _____

**Effortless Math Education**

# Answers – Chapter 7

## One–Step Equations

1) $x = 46$

2) $x = 24$

3) $x = 9$

4) $x = 53$

5) $x = 7$

6) $x = 13$

7) $x = -2$

8) $x = -18$

9) $x = -27$

10) $x = -10$

11) $x = 22$

12) $x = 9$

13) $x = 32$

14) $x = -26$

15) $x = -27$

16) $x = 25$

17) $x = 7$

18) $x = -3$

19) $x = -1$

20) $x = 3$

21) $x = -2$

22) $x = -10$

23) $x = 54$

24) $x = 135$

25) $x = -12$

26) $x = 56$

27) $x = -6$

28) $x = 7$

29) $x = 6$

30) $x = -5$

31) $x = -6$

## Multi –Step Equations

1) $x = 5$

2) $x = -22$

3) $x = 24$

4) $x = -21$

5) $x = -1$

6) $x = 6$

7) $x = -17$

8) $x = -3$

9) $x = -8$

10) $x = 15$

11) $x = -4$

12) $x = 4$

13) $x = -13$

14) $x = 1$

15) $x = 9$

16) $x = -1$

17) $x = 10$

18) $x = -3$

19) $x = -4$

20) $x = 0$

21) $x = -4$

22) $x = -1$

23) $x = -3$

24) $x = -2$

25) $x = -4$

26) $x = 1$

27) $x = -5$

28) $x = -8$

29) $x = -4$

30) $x = -5$

31) $x = -2$

32) $x = -19$

## System of Equations

1) $x = 6, y = 1$

2) $x = -4 , y = -1$

3) $x = 42, y = -12$

4) $x = 2 , y = 1$

5) $x = -\frac{11}{2} , y = -5$

6) $x = 1 , y = -2$

7) $x = 1 , y = 2$

8) $x = 1 , y = 1$

9) $x = 3 , y = 2$

10) $x = 3 , y = -2$

11) $x = 1, y = 2$

12) $x = 2, y = -5$

13) $x = 1, y = 2$

14) $x = -5, y = 8$

15) $x = 3, y = 2$

16) $x = -3 , y = -4$

## Graphing Single–Variable Inequalities

1) $x < 5$

2) $x \geq 2$

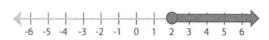

3) $x \geq -4$

4) $x \leq -1$

5) $x > -1$

6) $3 > x$

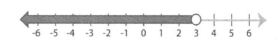

7) $2 \leq x$

8) $x > 0$

9) $-3 \leq x$

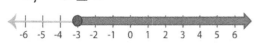

10) $-4 \leq x$

11) $x \leq 6$

12) $1 \leq x$

13) $-4 < x$

14) $x > -5$

## One–Step Inequalities

1) $x < 29$

2) $20 \leq x$

3) $x > 40$

4) $x \geq 8$

5) $x > 41$

6) $x \geq -2$

7) $x < -2$

8) $x \leq -18$

9) $x \geq -27$

10) $x < -13$

11) $22 \leq x$

12) $x > 4$

13) $x \geq 36$

14) $x > -25$

15) $x < -31$

16) $21 \leq x$

17) $x \leq 3$

18) $-4 \leq x$

19) $x > -7$

20) $x \leq 3$

21) $x < 2$

22) $x < -12$

23) $x > 36$

24) $108 \leq x$

25) $x < -24$

26) $x \geq 3$

27) $x \geq -5$

28) $x > 15$

29) $x \leq 8$

30) $x > 6$

31) $-7 < x$

## Multi –Step Inequalities

1) $x \leq 5$

2) $x \geq 5$

3) $x \geq 9$

4) $x \leq 12$

5) $x \leq 9$

6) $x \leq 8$

7) $x \leq 9$

8) $x \leq 4$

9) $x \leq 8$

10) $x \geq 11$

11) $x \geq 9$

12) $x < 5$

13) $x \geq 25$

14) $x < -7$

15) $x \geq 15$

16) $x \geq 8$

17) $x > -8$

18) $x \leq -11$

19) $x \geq 12$

20) $x \geq 3$

21) $x \leq 5$

22) $x \leq -4$

23) $x < 9$

24) $x < 3$

25) $x < 7$

26) $x \geq 3$

# Chapter 8: Lines and Slope

**Math Topics that you'll learn in this Chapter:**

- ✓ Finding Slope
- ✓ Graphing Lines Using Slope–Intercept Form
- ✓ Writing Linear Equations
- ✓ Graphing Linear Inequalities
- ✓ Finding Midpoint
- ✓ Finding Distance of Two Points

67

Chapter 8: Lines and Slope

## Finding Slope

✎ **Find the slope of each line.**

1) $y = 2x - 8$, Slope =

2) $y = -6x + 3$, Slope =

3) $y = -x - 5$, Slope =

4) $y = -2x - 9$, Slope =

5) $y = 5 + 2x$, Slope =

6) $y = 1 - 8x$, Slope =

7) $y = -4x + 3$, Slope =

8) $y = -9x + 8$, Slope =

9) $y = -2x + 4$, Slope =

10) $y = 9x - 8$, Slope =

11) $y = \frac{1}{2}x + 4$, Slope =

12) $y = -\frac{2}{5}x + 7$, Slope =

13) $-x + 3y = 5$, Slope =

14) $4x + 4y = 6$, Slope =

15) $6y - 2x = 10$, Slope =

16) $3y - x = 2$, Slope =

✎ **Find the slope of the line through each pair of points.**

17) $(4, 4), (8, 12)$, Slope =

23) $(8, 4), (9, 6)$, Slope =

18) $(-2, 4), (0, 6)$, Slope =

24) $(10, -1), (7, 8)$, Slope =

19) $(6, -2), (2, 6)$, Slope =

25) $(16, -3), (13, -6)$, Slope =

20) $(-4, -2), (0, 6)$, Slope =

26) $(12, 5), (8, 1)$, Slope =

21) $(6, 2), (3, 5)$, Slope =

27) $(6, 6), (8, 10)$, Slope =

22) $(-5, 1), (-1, 9)$, Slope =

28) $(10, -1), (8, 1)$, Slope =

# Graphing Lines Using Slope–Intercept Form

✏️ *Sketch the graph of each line.*

1) $y = -x + 1$

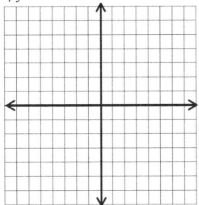

2) $y = 2x - 4$

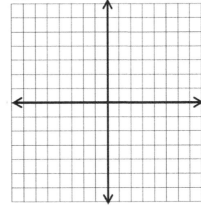

3) $y = -x + 6$

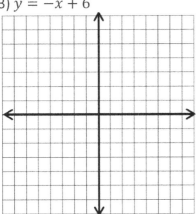

4) $y = x - 4$

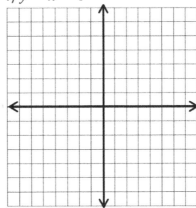

5) $y = 2x - 2$

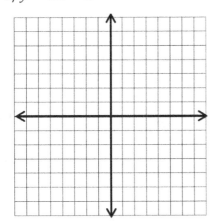

6) $y = -\frac{1}{2}x + 2$

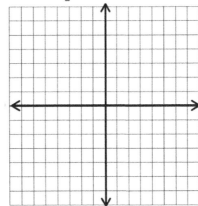

## Writing Linear Equations

✍️ *Write the equation of the line through the given points.*

1) through: $(2, -2), (3, 4)$     $y =$

2) through: $(-2, 4), (1, 7)$     $y =$

3) through: $(-1, 3), (3, 7)$     $y =$

4) through: $(6, 5), (3, 2)$     $y =$

5) through: $(7, -10), (2, 10)$  $y =$

6) through: $(7, 2), (6, 1)$     $y =$

7) through: $(6, -1), (4, 1)$    $y =$

8) through: $(-2, 8), (-4, -6)$  $y =$

9) through: $(-2, 5), (-3, 4)$     $y =$

10) through: $(6, 8), (8, -6)$     $y =$

11) through: $(-2, 5), (-4, -3)$   $y =$

12) through: $(8, 8), (4, -8)$     $y =$

13) through: $(7, -4)$, Slope: $-1$   $y =$

14) through: $(4, -10)$, Slope: $-2$  $y =$

15) through: $(6, 10)$, Slope: $9$    $y =$

16) through: $(-6, 8)$, Slope: $-2$   $y =$

✍️ *Solve each problem.*

17) What is the equation of a line with slope 6 and intercept 4? _____

18) What is the equation of a line with slope 5 and intercept 9? _____

19) What is the equation of a line with slope 8 and passes through point $(2, 8)$?

_____

20) What is the equation of a line with slope $-3$ and passes through point

$(-4, 10)$? _____

# Finding Midpoint

✒️ *Find the midpoint of the line segment with the given endpoints.*

1)  $(4,4),(0,4),$         midpoint = (__,__)

2)  $(5,1),(-1,5),$        midpoint = (__,__)

3)  $(4,-2),(0,6),$        midpoint = (__,__)

4)  $(-3,3),(-1,5),$       midpoint = (__,__)

5)  $(5,-2),(9,-6),$       midpoint = (__,__)

6)  $(-6,-3),(4,-7),$      midpoint = (__,__)

7)  $(7,0),(-7,8),$        midpoint = (__,__)

8)  $(-8,4),(-4,0),$       midpoint = (__,__)

9)  $(-3,6),(9,-8),$       midpoint = (__,__)

10) $(6,8),(6,-6),$        midpoint = (__,__)

11) $(6,7),(-8,5),$        midpoint = (__,__)

12) $(9,3),(-3,-9),$       midpoint = (__,__)

13) $(-6,12),(-4,6),$      midpoint = (__,__)

14) $(10,7),(8,-3),$       midpoint = (__,__)

15) $(13,7),(-5,3),$       midpoint = (__,__)

16) $(-9,-4),(-5,8),$      midpoint = (__,__)

17) $(12,5),(6,15),$       midpoint = (__,__)

18) $(-6,-10),(12,-2),$    midpoint = (__,__)

19) $(14,13),(-4,9),$      midpoint = (__,__)

20) $(10,-4),(8,12),$      midpoint = (__,__)

## Finding Distance of Two Points

✎ *Find the distance of each pair of points.*

1) $(0,9), (4,6)$,

   Distance = ____

2) $(-4,6), (8,11)$,

   Distance = ____

3) $(-6,1), (-3,5)$,

   Distance = ____

4) $(-3,2), (3,10)$,

   Distance = ____

5) $(-5,3), (4,-9)$,

   Distance = ____

6) $(-7,-5), (5,0)$,

   Distance = ____

7) $(4,3), (-4,-12)$,

   Distance = ____

8) $(10,1), (-5,-19)$,

   Distance = ____

9) $(3,3), (-1,5)$,

   Distance = ____

10) $(2,-1), (10,5)$,

   Distance = ____

11) $(-3,7), (-1,4)$,

   Distance = ____

12) $(5,-2), (9,-5)$,

   Distance = ____

13) $(-8,4), (4,9)$,

   Distance = ____

14) $(6,8), (6,-6)$,

   Distance = ____

15) $(6,-6), (0,2)$,

   Distance = ____

16) $(-4,10), (-4,4)$,

   Distance = ____

17) $(-7,-6), (-2,6)$,

   Distance = ____

18) $(11,0), (3,15)$,

   Distance = ____

# Answers – Chapter 8

## Finding Slope

| | | | | |
|---|---|---|---|---|
| 1) $2$ | 7) $-4$ | 13) $\frac{1}{3}$ | 18) $1$ | 24) $-3$ |
| 2) $-6$ | 8) $-9$ | 14) $-1$ | 19) $-2$ | 25) $1$ |
| 3) $-1$ | 9) $-2$ | 15) $\frac{1}{3}$ | 20) $2$ | 26) $1$ |
| 4) $-2$ | 10) $9$ | 16) $\frac{1}{3}$ | 21) $-1$ | 27) $2$ |
| 5) $2$ | 11) $\frac{1}{2}$ | 17) $2$ | 22) $2$ | 28) $-1$ |
| 6) $-8$ | 12) $-\frac{2}{5}$ | | 23) $2$ | |

## Graphing Lines Using Slope–Intercept Form

1) $y = -x + 1$

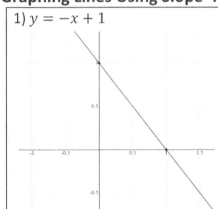

2) $y = 2x - 4$

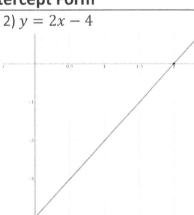

3) $y = -x + 6$

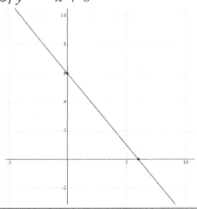

4) $y = x - 4$

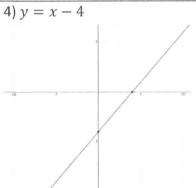

5) $y = 2x - 2$

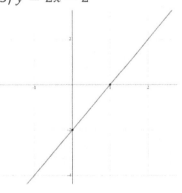

6) $y = -\frac{1}{2}x + 2$

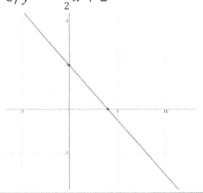

## Writing Linear Equations

1) $y = 6x - 14$

2) $y = x + 6$

3) $y = x + 4$

4) $y = x - 1$

5) $y = -4x + 18$

6) $y = x - 5$

7) $y = -x + 5$

8) $y = 7x + 22$

9) $y = x + 7$

10) $y = -7x + 50$

11) $y = 4x + 13$

12) $y = 4x - 24$

13) $y = -x + 3$

14) $y = -2x - 2$

15) $y = 9x - 44$

16) $y = -2x - 4$

17) $y = 6x + 4$

18) $y = 5x + 9$

19) $y = 8x - 8$

20) $y = -3x - 2$

## Finding Midpoint

1) $midpoint = (2, 4)$

2) $midpoint = (2, 3)$

3) $midpoint = (2, 2)$

4) $midpoint = (-2, 4)$

5) $midpoint = (7, -4)$

6) $midpoint = (-1, -5)$

7) $midpoint = (0, 4)$

8) $midpoint = (-6, 2)$

9) $midpoint = (3, -1)$

10) $midpoint = (6, 1)$

11) $midpoint = (-1, 6)$

12) $midpoint = (3, -3)$

13) $midpoint = (-5, 9)$

14) $midpoint = (9, 2)$

15) $midpoint = (4, 5)$

16) $midpoint = (-7, 2)$

17) $midpoint = (9, 10)$

18) $midpoint = (3, -6)$

19) $midpoint = (5, 11)$

20) $midpoint = (9, 4)$

## Finding Distance of Two Points

1) Distance = 5

2) Distance = 13

3) Distance = 5

4) Distance = 10

5) Distance = 15

6) Distance = 13

7) Distance = 17

8) Distance = 25

9) Distance = $\sqrt{20} = 2\sqrt{5}$

10) Distance = 10

11) Distance = $\sqrt{13}$

12) Distance = 5

13) Distance = 13

14) Distance = 14

15) Distance = 10

16) Distance = 6

17) Distance = 13

18) Distance = 17

# Chapter 9: Exponents and Variables

**Math Topics that you'll learn in this Chapter:**

- ✓ Multiplication Property of Exponents
- ✓ Division Property of Exponents
- ✓ Powers of Products and Quotients
- ✓ Zero and Negative Exponents
- ✓ Negative Exponents and Negative Bases
- ✓ Scientific Notation
- ✓ Radicals

# Multiplication Property of Exponents

✎ *Simplify and write the answer in exponential form.*

1) $3 \times 3^2 =$

2) $4^3 \times 4 =$

3) $2^2 \times 2^2 =$

4) $6^2 \times 6^2 =$

5) $7^3 \times 7^2 \times 7 =$

6) $2 \times 2^2 \times 2^2 =$

7) $5^3 \times 5^2 \times 5 \times 5 =$

8) $2x \times x =$

9) $x^3 \times x^2 =$

10) $x^4 \times x^4 =$

11) $x^2 \times x^2 \times x^2 =$

12) $6x \times 6x =$

13) $2x^2 \times 2x^2 =$

14) $3x^2 \times x =$

15) $4x^4 \times 4x^4 \times 4x^4 =$

16) $2x^2 \times x^2 =$

17) $x^4 \times 3x =$

18) $x \times 2x^2 =$

19) $5x^4 \times 5x^4 =$

20) $2yx^2 \times 2x =$

21) $3x^4 \times y^2x^4 =$

22) $y^2x^3 \times y^5x^2 =$

23) $4yx^3 \times 2x^2y^3 =$

24) $6x^2 \times 6x^3y^4 =$

25) $3x^4y^5 \times 7x^2y^3 =$

26) $7x^2y^5 \times 9xy^3 =$

27) $7xy^4 \times 4x^3y^3 =$

28) $3x^5y^3 \times 8x^2y^3 =$

29) $6x \times y^5x^2 \times y^3 =$

30) $yx^3 \times 3y^3x^2 \times 2xy =$

31) $5yx^3 \times 4y^2x \times xy^3 =$

32) $6x^2 \times 3x^3y^4 \times 10yx^3 =$

# Division Property of Exponents

✎ *Simplify and write the answer.*

1) $\dfrac{3^2}{3^3} =$

2) $\dfrac{2^6}{2^2} =$

3) $\dfrac{4^4}{4} =$

4) $\dfrac{5}{5^4} =$

5) $\dfrac{x}{x^3} =$

6) $\dfrac{3 \times 3^3}{3^2 \times 3^4} =$

7) $\dfrac{5^8}{5^3} =$

8) $\dfrac{5 \times 5^6}{5^2 \times 5^7} =$

9) $\dfrac{3^4 \times 3^7}{3^2 \times 3^8} =$

10) $\dfrac{5x}{10x^3} =$

11) $\dfrac{5x^3}{2x^5} =$

12) $\dfrac{18x^3}{14x^6} =$

13) $\dfrac{12x^3}{8xy^8} =$

14) $\dfrac{24xy^3}{4x^4y^2} =$

15) $\dfrac{21x^3y^9}{7xy^5} =$

16) $\dfrac{36x^2y^9}{4x^3} =$

17) $\dfrac{18x^3y^4}{10x^6y^8} =$

18) $\dfrac{16y^2x^{14}}{24yx^8} =$

19) $\dfrac{15x^4y}{9x^9y^2} =$

20) $\dfrac{7x^7y^2}{28x^5y^6} =$

# Powers of Products and Quotients

✍ *Simplify and write the answer.*

1) $(3^2)^2 =$

2) $(5^2)^3 =$

3) $(3 \times 3^3)^4 =$

4) $(6 \times 6^4)^2 =$

5) $(3^3 \times 3^2)^3 =$

6) $(5^4 \times 5^5)^2 =$

7) $(2 \times 2^4)^2 =$

8) $(2x^6)^2 =$

9) $(11x^5)^2 =$

10) $(4x^2y^4)^4 =$

11) $(2x^4y^4)^3 =$

12) $(3x^2y^2)^2 =$

13) $(3x^4y^3)^4 =$

14) $(2x^6y^8)^2 =$

15) $(12x^3x)^3 =$

16) $(5x^9x^6)^3 =$

17) $(5x^{10}y^3)^3 =$

18) $(14x^3x^3)^2 =$

19) $(3x^35x)^2 =$

20) $(10x^{11}y^3)^2 =$

21) $(9x^7y^5)^2 =$

22) $(4x^4y^6)^5 =$

23) $(3x4y^3)^2 =$

24) $\left(\frac{6x}{x^2}\right)^2 =$

25) $\left(\frac{x^5y^5}{x^2y^2}\right)^3 =$

26) $\left(\frac{24x}{4x^6}\right)^2 =$

27) $\left(\frac{x^5}{x^6y^2}\right)^2 =$

28) $\left(\frac{xy^3}{x^2y^5}\right)^3 =$

29) $\left(\frac{3xy^3}{x^4}\right)^2 =$

30) $\left(\frac{xy^5}{4xy^3}\right)^3 =$

# Zero and Negative Exponents

✎ *Evaluate the following expressions.*

1) $2^{-1} =$

2) $3^{-2} =$

3) $0^{10} =$

4) $1^{-8} =$

5) $8^{-1} =$

6) $8^{-2} =$

7) $2^{-4} =$

8) $10^{-2} =$

9) $9^{-2} =$

10) $3^{-3} =$

11) $7^{-3} =$

12) $3^{-4} =$

13) $6^{-3} =$

14) $5^{-3} =$

15) $22^{-1} =$

16) $4^{-4} =$

17) $5^{-4} =$

18) $15^{-2} =$

19) $4^{-5} =$

20) $9^{-3} =$

21) $3^{-5} =$

22) $5^{-4} =$

23) $12^{-2} =$

24) $15^{-3} =$

25) $20^{-3} =$

26) $50^{-2} =$

27) $18^{-3} =$

28) $24^{-2} =$

29) $30^{-3} =$

30) $10^{-5} =$

31) $\left(\frac{1}{8}\right)^{-1} =$

32) $\left(\frac{1}{5}\right)^{-2} =$

33) $\left(\frac{1}{7}\right)^{-2} =$

34) $\left(\frac{2}{3}\right)^{-2} =$

35) $\left(\frac{1}{5}\right)^{-3} =$

36) $\left(\frac{3}{4}\right)^{-2} =$

37) $\left(\frac{2}{5}\right)^{-2} =$

38) $\left(\frac{1}{2}\right)^{-8} =$

39) $\left(\frac{2}{3}\right)^{-3} =$

40) $\left(\frac{3}{4}\right)^{-3} =$

41) $\left(\frac{5}{6}\right)^{-2} =$

42) $\left(\frac{6}{9}\right)^{-2} =$

# Negative Exponents and Negative Bases

✎ *Simplify and write the answer.*

1) $-2^{-1} =$

2) $-4^{-2} =$

3) $-3^{-4} =$

4) $-x^{-5} =$

5) $2x^{-1} =$

6) $-4x^{-3} =$

7) $-12x^{-5} =$

8) $-5x^{-2}y^{-3} =$

9) $20x^{-4}y^{-1} =$

10) $14a^{-6}b^{-7} =$

11) $-12x^2y^{-3} =$

12) $-\dfrac{25}{x^{-6}} =$

13) $-\dfrac{2x}{y^{-4}} =$

14) $\left(-\dfrac{1}{3x}\right)^{-2} =$

15) $\left(-\dfrac{3}{4x}\right)^{-2} =$

16) $-\dfrac{9}{a^{-7}b^{-2}} =$

17) $-\dfrac{5x}{x^{-3}} =$

18) $-\dfrac{a^{-3}}{b^{-2}} =$

19) $-\dfrac{8}{x^{-3}} =$

20) $\dfrac{5b}{-9c^{-4}} =$

21) $\dfrac{9ab}{a^{-3}b^{-1}} =$

22) $-\dfrac{15a^{-2}}{30b^{-3}} =$

23) $\dfrac{4ab^{-2}}{-3c^{-2}} =$

24) $\left(\dfrac{3a}{2c}\right)^{-2} =$

25) $\left(-\dfrac{3x}{4yz}\right)^{-2} =$

26) $\dfrac{15ab^{-6}}{-9c^{-2}} =$

27) $\left(-\dfrac{x^3}{x^4}\right)^{-3} =$

28) $\left(-\dfrac{x^{-2}}{2x^2}\right)^{-2} =$

## Scientific Notation

✎ **Write each number in scientific notation.**

1) $0.114 =$

2) $0.06 =$

3) $8.6 =$

4) $30 =$

5) $60 =$

6) $0.004 =$

7) $78 =$

8) $1,600 =$

9) $1,450 =$

10) $31,000 =$

11) $2,000,000 =$

12) $0.0000003 =$

13) $554,000 =$

14) $0.000725 =$

15) $0.00034 =$

16) $86,000,000 =$

17) $62,000 =$

18) $97,000,000 =$

19) $0.0000045 =$

20) $0.0019 =$

✎ **Write each number in standard notation.**

21) $2 \times 10^{-1} =$

22) $8 \times 10^{-2} =$

23) $1.8 \times 10^{3} =$

24) $9 \times 10^{-4} =$

25) $1.7 \times 10^{-2} =$

26) $9 \times 10^{3} =$

27) $6 \times 10^{4} =$

28) $2.18 \times 10^{5} =$

29) $5 \times 10^{-3} =$

30) $9.4 \times 10^{-5} =$

## Radicals

✏️ *Simplify and write the answer.*

1) $\sqrt{1} =$ ___

2) $\sqrt{0} =$ ___

3) $\sqrt{16} =$ ___

4) $\sqrt{4} =$ ___

5) $\sqrt{9} =$ ___

6) $\sqrt{25} =$ ___

7) $\sqrt{49} =$ ___

8) $\sqrt{36} =$ ___

9) $\sqrt{64} =$ ___

10) $\sqrt{81} =$ ___

11) $\sqrt{121} =$ ___

12) $\sqrt{225} =$ ___

13) $\sqrt{144} =$ ___

14) $\sqrt{100} =$ ___

15) $\sqrt{256} =$ ___

16) $\sqrt{289} =$ ___

17) $\sqrt{324} =$ ___

18) $\sqrt{400} =$ ___

19) $\sqrt{900} =$ ___

20) $\sqrt{529} =$ ___

21) $\sqrt{361} =$ ___

22) $\sqrt{169} =$ ___

23) $\sqrt{196} =$ ___

24) $\sqrt{90} =$ ___

✏️ *Evaluate.*

25) $\sqrt{6} \times \sqrt{6} =$

26) $\sqrt{5} \times \sqrt{5} =$

27) $\sqrt{8} \times \sqrt{8} =$

28) $\sqrt{2} + \sqrt{2} =$

29) $\sqrt{8} + \sqrt{8} =$

30) $6\sqrt{5} - 2\sqrt{5} =$

31) $\sqrt{25} \times \sqrt{16} =$

32) $\sqrt{25} \times \sqrt{64} =$

33) $\sqrt{64} \times \sqrt{49} =$

34) $5\sqrt{5} \times 3\sqrt{5} =$

35) $7\sqrt{3} \times 2\sqrt{3} =$

36) $5\sqrt{2} - \sqrt{8} =$

**Effortless Math Education**

# Answers – Chapter 9

## Multiplication Property of Exponents

1) $3^3$

2) $4^4$

3) $2^4$

4) $6^4$

5) $7^6$

6) $2^5$

7) $5^7$

8) $2x^2$

9) $x^5$

10) $x^8$

11) $x^6$

12) $36x^2$

13) $4x^4$

14) $3x^3$

15) $64x^{12}$

16) $2x^4$

17) $3x^5$

18) $2x^3$

19) $25x^8$

20) $4x^3y$

21) $3x^8y^2$

22) $x^5y^7$

23) $8x^5y^4$

24) $36x^5y^4$

25) $21x^6y^8$

26) $63x^3y^8$

27) $28x^4y^7$

28) $24x^7y^6$

29) $6x^3y^8$

30) $6x^6y^5$

31) $20x^5y^6$

32) $180x^8y^5$

## Division Property of Exponents

1) $\frac{1}{3}$

2) $2^4$

3) $4^3$

4) $\frac{1}{5^3}$

5) $\frac{1}{x^2}$

6) $\frac{1}{3^2}$

7) $5^5$

8) $\frac{1}{5^2}$

9) $3$

10) $\frac{1}{2x^2}$

11) $\frac{5}{2x^2}$

12) $\frac{9}{7x^3}$

13) $\frac{3x^2}{2y^8}$

14) $\frac{6y}{x^3}$

15) $3x^2y^4$

16) $\frac{9y^9}{x}$

17) $\frac{9}{5x^3y^4}$

18) $\frac{2yx^6}{3}$

19) $\frac{5}{3x^5y}$

20) $\frac{x^2}{4y^4}$

## Powers of Products and Quotients

1) $3^4$

2) $5^6$

3) $3^{16}$

4) $6^{10}$

5) $3^{15}$

6) $5^{18}$

7) $2^{10}$

8) $4x^{12}$

9) $121x^{10}$

10) $256x^8y^{16}$

11) $8x^{12}y^{12}$

12) $9x^4y^4$

13) $81x^{16}y^{12}$

14) $4x^{12}y^{16}$

15) $1,728x^{12}$

16) $125x^{45}$

17) $125x^{30}y^9$

18) $196x^{12}$

19) $225x^8$

20) $100x^{22}y^6$

21) $81x^{14}y^{10}$

22) $1,024x^{20}y^{30}$

23) $144x^2y^6$

24) $\dfrac{36}{x^2}$

25) $x^9y^9$

26) $\dfrac{36}{x^{10}}$

27) $\dfrac{1}{x^2y^4}$

28) $\dfrac{1}{x^3y^6}$

29) $\dfrac{9y^6}{x^6}$

30) $\dfrac{y^6}{64}$

## Zero and Negative Exponents

1) $\frac{1}{2}$

2) $\frac{1}{9}$

3) $0$

4) $1$

5) $\frac{1}{8}$

6) $\frac{1}{64}$

7) $\frac{1}{16}$

8) $\frac{1}{100}$

9) $\frac{1}{81}$

10) $\frac{1}{27}$

11) $\frac{1}{343}$

12) $\frac{1}{81}$

13) $\frac{1}{216}$

14) $\frac{1}{125}$

15) $\frac{1}{22}$

16) $\frac{1}{256}$

17) $\frac{1}{625}$

18) $\frac{1}{225}$

19) $\frac{1}{1,024}$

20) $\frac{1}{729}$

21) $\frac{1}{243}$

22) $\frac{1}{625}$

23) $\frac{1}{144}$

24) $\frac{1}{3,375}$

25) $\frac{1}{8,000}$

26) $\frac{1}{2,500}$

27) $\frac{1}{5,832}$

28) $\frac{1}{576}$

29) $\frac{1}{27,000}$

30) $\frac{1}{100,000}$

31) $8$

32) $25$

33) $49$

34) $\frac{9}{4}$

35) $125$

36) $\frac{16}{9}$

37) $\frac{25}{4}$

38) $256$

39) $\frac{27}{8}$

40) $\frac{64}{27}$

41) $\frac{36}{25}$

42) $\frac{81}{36}$

## Negative Exponents and Negative Bases

1) $-\dfrac{1}{2}$

2) $-\dfrac{1}{16}$

3) $-\dfrac{1}{81}$

4) $-\dfrac{1}{x^5}$

5) $\dfrac{2}{x}$

6) $-\dfrac{4}{x^3}$

7) $-\dfrac{12}{x^5}$

8) $-\dfrac{5}{x^2 y^3}$

9) $\dfrac{20}{x^4 y}$

10) $\dfrac{14}{a^6 b^7}$

11) $-\dfrac{12x^2}{y^3}$

12) $-25x^6$

13) $-2xy^4$

14) $9x^2$

15) $\dfrac{16x^2}{9}$

16) $-9a^7 b^2$

17) $-5x^4$

18) $-\dfrac{b^2}{a^3}$

19) $-8x^3$

20) $-\dfrac{5bc^4}{9}$

21) $9a^4 b^2$

22) $-\dfrac{b^3}{2a^2}$

23) $-\dfrac{4ac^2}{3b^2}$

24) $\dfrac{4c^2}{9a^2}$

25) $\dfrac{16y^2 z^2}{9x^2}$

26) $-\dfrac{5ac^2}{3b^6}$

27) $-x^3$

28) $4x^8$

## Scientific Notation

1) $1.14 \times 10^{-1}$

2) $6 \times 10^{-2}$

3) $8.6 \times 10^0$

4) $3 \times 10^1$

5) $6 \times 10^1$

6) $4 \times 10^{-3}$

7) $7.8 \times 10^1$

8) $1.6 \times 10^3$

9) $1.45 \times 10^3$

10) $3.1 \times 10^4$

11) $2 \times 10^6$

12) $3 \times 10^{-7}$

13) $5.54 \times 10^5$

14) $7.25 \times 10^{-4}$

15) $3.4 \times 10^{-4}$

16) $8.6 \times 10^7$

17) $6.2 \times 10^4$

18) $9.7 \times 10^7$

19) $4.5 \times 10^{-6}$

20) $1.9 \times 10^{-3}$

21) $0.2$

22) $0.08$

23) $1,800$

24) $0.0009$

25) $0.017$

26) $9,000$

27) $60,000$

28) $218,000$

29) $0.005$

30) $0.000094$

**Radicals**

1) 1

2) 0

3) 4

4) 2

5) 3

6) 5

7) 7

8) 6

9) 8

10) 9

11) 11

12) 15

13) 12

14) 10

15) 16

16) 17

17) 18

18) 20

19) 30

20) 23

21) 19

22) 13

23) 14

24) $3\sqrt{10}$

25) 6

26) 5

27) 8

28) $2\sqrt{2}$

29) $2\sqrt{8} = 4\sqrt{2}$

30) $4\sqrt{5}$

31) 20

32) 40

33) 56

34) 75

35) 42

36) $3\sqrt{2}$

# Chapter 10:
# Polynomials

**Math Topics that you'll learn in this Chapter:**

- ✓ Simplifying Polynomials
- ✓ Adding and Subtracting Polynomials
- ✓ Multiplying Monomials
- ✓ Multiplying and Dividing Monomials
- ✓ Multiplying a Polynomial and a Monomial
- ✓ Multiplying Binomials
- ✓ Factoring Trinomials

91

## Simplifying Polynomials

✎ *Simplify each expression.*

1) $3(2x + 1) =$ _____

2) $2(4x - 6) =$ _____

3) $4(3x + 3) =$ _____

4) $2(4x + 5) =$ _____

5) $-3(8x - 7) =$ _____

6) $2x(3x + 4) =$ _____

7) $3x^2 + 3x^2 - 2x^3 =$ _____

8) $2x - x^2 + 6x^3 + 4 =$ _____

9) $5x + 2x^2 - 9x^3 =$ _____

10) $7x^2 + 5x^4 - 2x^3 =$ _____

11) $-3x^2 + 5x^3 + 6x^4 =$ _____

12) $(x - 3)(x - 4) =$ _____

13) $(x - 5)(x + 4) =$ _____

14) $(x - 6)(x - 3) =$ _____

15) $(2x + 5)(x + 8) =$ _____

16) $(3x - 8)(x + 4) =$ _____

17) $-8x^2 + 2x^3 - 10x^4 + 5x =$ _____

18) $11 - 6x^2 + 5x^2 - 12x^3 + 22 =$ _____

19) $3x^2 - 4x + 4x^3 + 10x - 21x =$ _____

20) $10 - 6x^2 + 5x^2 - 3x^3 + 2 =$ _____

21) $3x^5 - 2x^3 + 8x^2 - x^5 =$ _____

22) $(5x^3 - 1) + (4x^3 - 6x^3) =$ _____

**Chapter 10: Polynomials**

# Adding and Subtracting Polynomials

✍ *Add or subtract expressions.*

1) $(x^2 - 5) + (x^2 + 6) =$ _____

2) $(2x^2 - 6) - (3 - 2x^2) =$ _____

3) $(x^3 + 3x^2) - (x^3 + 6) =$ _____

4) $(4x^3 - x^2) + (6x^2 - 8x) =$ _____

5) $(2x^3 + 3x) - (5x^3 + 2) =$ _____

6) $(5x^3 - 2) + (2x^3 + 10) =$ _____

7) $(7x^3 + 5) - (9 - 4x^3) =$ _____

8) $(5x^2 + 3x^3) - (2x^3 + 6) =$ _____

9) $(8x^2 - x) + (4x - 8x^2) =$ _____

10) $(6x + 9x^2) - (5x + 2) =$ _____

11) $(7x^4 - 2x) - (6x - 2x^4) =$ _____

12) $(2x - 4x^3) - (9x^3 + 6x) =$ _____

13) $(8x^3 - 8x^2) - (6x^2 - 3x) =$ _____

14) $(9x^2 - 6) + (5x^2 - 4x^3) =$ _____

15) $(8x^3 + 3x^4) - (x^4 - 3x^3) =$ _____

16) $(-4x^3 - 2x) + (5x - 2x^3) =$ _____

17) $(9x - 5x^4) - (8x^4 + 4x) =$ _____

18) $(8x - 3x^2) - (7x^4 - 3x^2) =$ _____

19) $(9x^3 - 7) + (5x^3 - 4x^2) =$ _____

20) $(7x^3 + x^4) - (6x^4 - 5x^3) =$ _____

## Multiplying Monomials

✎ *Simplify each expression.*

1) $4x^7 \times x^3 =$

_____

2) $6y^2 \times 6y^3 =$

_____

3) $-6z^7 \times 4z^4 =$

_____

4) $5x^5y \times 8xy^3 =$

_____

5) $-6xy^8 \times 3x^5y^3 =$

_____

6) $7a^4b^2 \times 3a^8b =$

_____

7) $5xy^5 \times 3x^3y^4 =$

_____

8) $5p^5q^4 \times (-6pq^4) =$

_____

9) $8s^6t^2 \times 6s^3t^7 =$

_____

10) $(-8x^5y^2) \times 4x^6y^3 =$

_____

11) $9xy^6z \times 3y^4z^2 =$

_____

12) $12x^5y^4 \times 2x^8y =$

_____

13) $4pq^5 \times (-7p^4q^8) =$

_____

14) $9s^4t^2 \times (-5st^5) =$

_____

15) $10p^3q^5 \times (-4p^4q^6) =$

_____

16) $(-5p^2q^4r) \times 7pq^5r^3 =$

_____

17) $(-9a^4b^7c^4) \times (-4a^7b) =$

_____

18) $7u^5v^9 \times (-5u^{12}v^7) =$

_____

19) $4u^4v^9z^2 \times (-5uv^8z) =$

_____

20) $(-6xy^3z^5) \times 3x^3yz^7 =$

_____

21) $6x^2y^3z^5 \times (-7x^4y^2z) =$

_____

22) $7a^5b^8c^{12} \times 4a^6b^5c^9 =$

_____

# Multiplying and Dividing Monomials

✎ *Simplify each expression.*

1) $(3x^5)(2x^2) =$

_____

2) $(6x^5)(2x^4) =$

_____

3) $(-7x^9)(2x^5) =$

_____

4) $(7x^7y^9)(-5x^6y^6) =$

_____

5) $(8x^5y^6)(3x^2y^5) =$

_____

6) $(8yx^2)(7y^5x^3) =$

_____

7) $(4x^2y)(2x^2y^3) =$

_____

8) $(-2x^9y^4)(-9x^6y^8) =$

_____

9) $(-5x^8y^2)(-6x^4y^5) =$

_____

10) $(8x^8y)(-7x^4y^3) =$

_____

11) $(9x^6y^2)(6x^7y^4) =$

_____

12) $(8x^9y^5)(6x^5y^4) =$

_____

13) $(-5x^8y^9)(7x^7y^8) =$

_____

14) $(6x^2y^5)(5x^3y^2) =$

_____

15) $(9x^5y^{12})(4x^7y^9) =$

_____

16) $(-10x^{14}y^8)(2x^7y^5) =$

_____

17) $\frac{6x^5y^7}{xy^6} =$

_____

18) $\frac{9x^6y^6}{3x^4y} =$

_____

19) $\frac{16x^4y^6}{4xy} =$

_____

20) $\frac{-30x^9y^8}{5x^5y^4} =$

_____

# Multiplying a Polynomial and a Monomial

✎ *Find each product.*

1) $x(x - 5) =$

_____

2) $2(3 + x) =$

_____

3) $x(x - 7) =$

_____

4) $x(x + 9) =$

_____

5) $2x(x - 2) =$

_____

6) $5(4x + 3) =$

_____

7) $4x(3x - 4) =$

_____

8) $x(5x + 2y) =$

_____

9) $3x(x - 2y) =$

_____

10) $6x(3x - 4y) =$

_____

11) $2x(3x - 8) =$

_____

12) $6x(4x - 6y) =$

_____

13) $3x(4x - 2y) =$

_____

14) $2x(2x - 6y) =$

_____

15) $5x(x^2 + y^2) =$

_____

16) $3x(2x^2 - y^2) =$

_____

17) $6(9x^2 + 3y^2) =$

_____

18) $4x(-3x^2y + 2y) =$

_____

19) $-3(6x^2 - 5xy + 3) =$

_____

20) $6(x^2 - 4xy - 3) =$

_____

# Multiplying Binomials

✎ *Find each product.*

1) $(x - 3)(x + 4) =$

_____

2) $(x + 3)(x + 5) =$

_____

3) $(x - 6)(x - 7) =$

_____

4) $(x - 9)(x - 4) =$

_____

5) $(x - 7)(x - 5) =$

_____

6) $(x + 6)(x + 2) =$

_____

7) $(x - 9)(x + 3) =$

_____

8) $(x - 8)(x - 5) =$

_____

9) $(x + 3)(x + 7) =$

_____

10) $(x - 9)(x + 4) =$

_____

11) $(x + 6)(x + 6) =$

_____

12) $(x + 7)(x + 7) =$

_____

13) $(x - 8)(x + 7) =$

_____

14) $(x + 9)(x + 9) =$

_____

15) $(x - 8)(x - 8) =$

_____

16) $(x - 9)(x + 5) =$

_____

17) $(2x - 5)(x + 4) =$

_____

18) $(2x + 6)(x + 3) =$

_____

19) $(2x + 4)(x + 5) =$

_____

20) $(2x - 3)(2x + 2) =$

_____

# Factoring Trinomials

✎ *Factor each trinomial.*

1) $x^2 + 5x + 4 =$

_____

2) $x^2 + 5x + 6 =$

_____

3) $x^2 - 4x + 3 =$

_____

4) $x^2 - 10x + 25 =$

_____

5) $x^2 - 13x + 40 =$

_____

6) $x^2 + 8x + 12 =$

_____

7) $x^2 - 6x - 27 =$

_____

8) $x^2 - 14x + 48 =$

_____

9) $x^2 + 15x + 56 =$

_____

10) $x^2 - 5x - 36 =$

_____

11) $x^2 + 12x + 36 =$

_____

12) $x^2 + 16x + 63 =$

_____

13) $x^2 + x - 72 =$

_____

14) $x^2 + 18x + 81 =$

_____

15) $x^2 - 16x + 64 =$

_____

16) $x^2 - 18x + 81 =$

_____

17) $2x^2 + 10x + 8 =$

_____

18) $2x^2 + 4x - 6 =$

_____

19) $2x^2 + 9x + 4 =$

_____

20) $4x^2 + 4x - 24 =$

_____

# Answers – Chapter 10

**Simplifying Polynomials**

1) $6x + 3$

2) $8x - 12$

3) $12x + 12$

4) $8x + 10$

5) $-24x + 21$

6) $6x^2 + 8x$

7) $-2x^3 + 6x^2$

8) $6x^3 - x^2 + 2x + 4$

9) $-9x^3 + 2x^2 + 5x$

10) $5x^4 - 2x^3 + 7x^2$

11) $6x^4 + 5x^3 - 3x^2$

12) $x^2 - 7x + 12$

13) $x^2 - x - 20$

14) $x^2 - 9x + 18$

15) $2x^2 + 21x + 40$

16) $3x^2 + 4x - 32$

17) $-10x^4 + 2x^3 - 8x^2 + 5x$

18) $-12x^3 - x^2 + 33$

19) $4x^3 + 3x^2 - 15x$

20) $-3x^3 - x^2 + 12$

21) $2x^5 - 2x^3 + 8x^2$

22) $3x^3 - 1$

## Adding and Subtracting Polynomials

1) $2x^2 + 1$

2) $4x^2 - 9$

3) $3x^2 - 6$

4) $4x^3 + 5x^2 - 8x$

5) $-3x^3 + 3x - 2$

6) $7x^3 + 8$

7) $11x^3 - 4$

8) $x^3 + 5x^2 - 6$

9) $3x$

10) $9x^2 + x - 2$

11) $9x^4 - 8x$

12) $-13x^3 - 4x$

13) $8x^3 - 14x^2 + 3x$

14) $-4x^3 + 14x^2 - 6$

15) $2x^4 + 11x^3$

16) $-6x^3 + 3x$

17) $-13x^4 + 5x$

18) $-7x^4 + 8x$

19) $14x^3 - 4x^2 - 7$

20) $-5x^4 + 12x^3$

## Multiplying Monomials

1) $4x^{10}$

2) $36y^5$

3) $-24z^{11}$

4) $40x^6y^4$

5) $-18x^6y^{11}$

6) $21a^{12}b^3$

7) $15x^4y^9$

8) $-30p^6q^8$

9) $48s^9t^9$

10) $-32x^{11}y^5$

11) $27xy^{10}z^3$

12) $24x^{13}y^5$

13) $-28p^5q^{13}$

14) $-45s^5t^7$

15) $-40p^7q^{11}$

16) $-35p^3q^9r^4$

17) $36a^{11}b^8c^4$

18) $-35u^{17}v^{16}$

19) $-20u^5v^{17}z^3$

20) $-18x^4y^4z^{12}$

21) $-42x^6y^5z^6$

22) $28a^{11}b^{13}c^{21}$

## Multiplying and Dividing Monomials

1) $6x^7$

2) $12x^9$

3) $-14x^{14}$

4) $-35x^{13}y^{15}$

5) $24x^7y^{11}$

6) $56y^6x^5$

7) $8x^4y^4$

8) $18x^{15}y^{12}$

9) $30x^{12}y^7$

10) $-56x^{12}y^4$

11) $54x^{13}y^6$

12) $48x^{14}y^9$

13) $-35x^{15}y^{17}$

14) $30x^5y^7$

15) $36x^{12}y^{21}$

16) $-20x^{21}y^{13}$

17) $6x^4y$

18) $3x^2y^5$

19) $4x^3y^5$

20) $-6x^4y^4$

## Multiplying a Polynomial and a Monomial

1) $x^2 - 5x$

2) $2x + 6$

3) $x^2 - 7x$

4) $x^2 + 9x$

5) $2x^2 - 4x$

6) $20x + 15$

7) $12x^2 - 16x$

8) $5x^2 + 2xy$

9) $3x^2 - 6xy$

10) $18x^2 - 24xy$

11) $6x^2 - 16x$

12) $24x^2 - 36xy$

13) $12x^2 - 6xy$

14) $4x^2 - 12xy$

15) $5x^3 + 5xy^2$

16) $6x^3 - 3xy^2$

17) $54x^2 + 18y^2$

18) $-12x^3y + 8xy$

19) $-18x^2 + 15xy - 9$

20) $6x^2 - 24xy - 18$

## Multiplying Binomials

1) $x^2 + x - 12$

2) $x^2 + 8x + 15$

3) $x^2 - 13x + 42$

4) $x^2 - 13x + 36$

5) $x^2 - 12x + 35$

6) $x^2 + 8x + 12$

7) $x^2 - 6x - 27$

8) $x^2 - 13x + 40$

9) $x^2 + 10x + 21$

10) $x^2 - 5x - 36$

11) $x^2 + 12x + 36$

12) $x^2 + 14x + 49$

13) $x^2 - x - 56$

14) $x^2 + 18x + 81$

15) $x^2 - 16x + 64$

16) $x^2 - 4x - 45$

17) $2x^2 + 3x - 20$

18) $2x^2 + 12x + 18$

19) $2x^2 + 14x + 20$

20) $4x^2 - 2x - 6$

Effortless
Math
Education

**Factoring Trinomials**

1) $(x + 4)(x + 1)$

2) $(x + 3)(x + 2)$

3) $(x - 1)(x - 3)$

4) $(x - 5)(x - 5)$

5) $(x - 8)(x - 5)$

6) $(x + 6)(x + 2)$

7) $(x - 9)(x + 3)$

8) $(x - 8)(x - 6)$

9) $(x + 8)(x + 7)$

10) $(x - 9)(x + 4)$

11) $(x + 6)(x + 6)$

12) $(x + 7)(x + 9)$

13) $(x - 8)(x + 9)$

14) $(x + 9)(x + 9)$

15) $(x - 8)(x - 8)$

16) $(x - 9)(x - 9)$

17) $2(x + 1)(x + 4)$

18) $2(x - 1)(x + 3)$

19) $(2x + 1)(x + 4)$

20) $(2x - 4)(2x + 6)$

# Chapter 11: Geometry and Solid Figures

**Math Topics that you'll learn in this Chapter:**

- ✓ The Pythagorean Theorem
- ✓ Triangles
- ✓ Polygons
- ✓ Circles
- ✓ Trapezoids
- ✓ Cubes
- ✓ Rectangle Prisms
- ✓ Cylinder

# The Pythagorean Theorem

 *Do the following lengths form a right triangle?*

1) _____

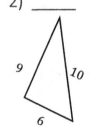

2) _____

3) _____

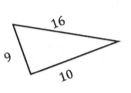

4) _____

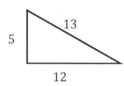

5) _____

6) _____

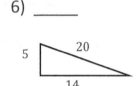

7) _____

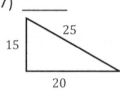

8) _____

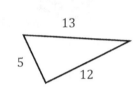

*Find the missing side.*

9) _____

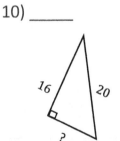

10) _____

11) _____

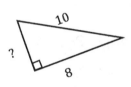

12) _____

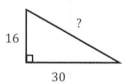

13) _____

14) _____

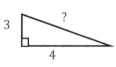

15) _____

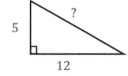

16) _____

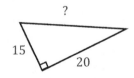

# Triangles

✎ *Find the measure of the unknown angle in each triangle.*

1) _____

85°
88°
? °

2) _____

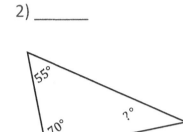
55°
70°
? °

3) _____

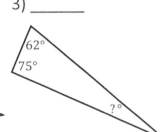
62°
75°
? °

4) _____

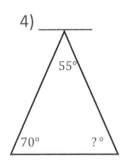
55°
70°     ? °

5) _____

55°
80°     ? °

6) _____

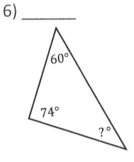
60°
74°
? °

7) _____

? °
43°
85°

8) _____

35°
74°   ? °

✎ *Find area of each triangle.*

9) _____

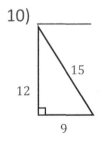
6
9

10) _____

15
12
9

11) _____

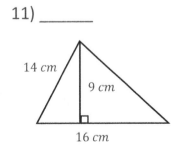
14 cm
9 cm
16 cm

12) _____

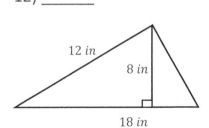
12 in
8 in
18 in

**Chapter 11: Geometry and Solid Figures**

## Polygons

✎ *Find the perimeter of each shape.*

1) (square) _____

6 cm

2) _____

12 m
8 m     8 m
12 m

3) _____

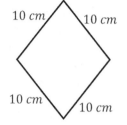

10 cm   10 cm
10 cm   10 cm

4) (square) _____

8 m

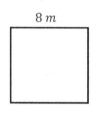

5) (regular hexagon)

_____

16 m

6) _____

14 m
12 m     12 m
18 m

7) (parallelogram)

_____

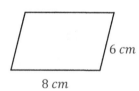

8 cm   6 cm

8) (regular hexagon)

_____

20 ft

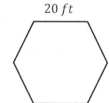

9) _____

16 ft
16 ft     16 ft
16 ft

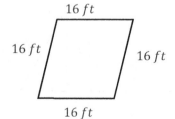

10) _____

22 in
18 in     18 in
22 in

11) _____

15 ft   15 ft
15 ft   15 ft

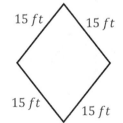

12) (regular hexagon)

_____

30 in

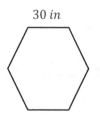

## Circles

✍ **Find the Circumference of each circle.** ($\pi = 3.14$)

1) _____    2) _____    3) _____    4) _____    5) _____    6) _____

7) _____    8) _____    9) _____    10) _____    11) _____    12) _____

✍ **Complete the table below.** ($\pi = 3.14$)

| | Radius | Diameter | Circumference | Area |
|---|---|---|---|---|
| **Circle 1** | 2 inches | 4 inches | 12.56 inches | 12.56 square inches |
| **Circle 2** | | 8 meters | | |
| **Circle 3** | | | | 113.04 square feet |
| **Circle 4** | | | 50.24 miles | |
| **Circle 5** | | 9 kilometers | | |
| **Circle 6** | 7 centimeters | | | |
| **Circle 7** | | 18 feet | | |
| **Circle 8** | | | | 78.5 square meters |
| **Circle 9** | | | 69.08 inches | |
| **Circle 10** | 10 feet | | | |

## Cubes

✎ *Find the volume of each cube.*

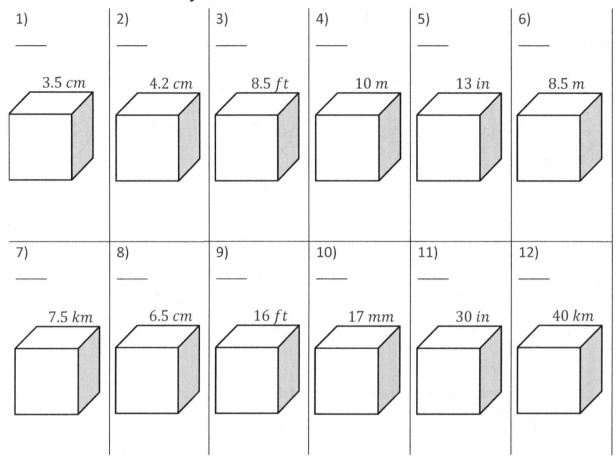

| 1) ___ | 2) ___ | 3) ___ | 4) ___ | 5) ___ | 6) ___ |
|---|---|---|---|---|---|
| 3.5 cm | 4.2 cm | 8.5 ft | 10 m | 13 in | 8.5 m |

| 7) ___ | 8) ___ | 9) ___ | 10) ___ | 11) ___ | 12) ___ |
|---|---|---|---|---|---|
| 7.5 km | 6.5 cm | 16 ft | 17 mm | 30 in | 40 km |

✎ *Find the surface area of each cube.*

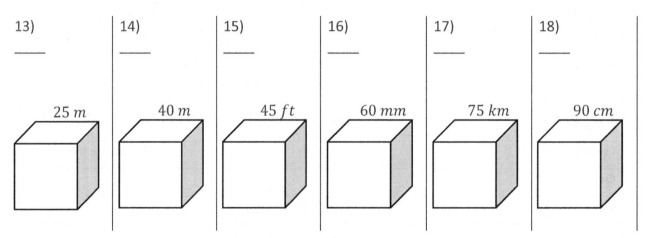

| 13) ___ | 14) ___ | 15) ___ | 16) ___ | 17) ___ | 18) ___ |
|---|---|---|---|---|---|
| 25 m | 40 m | 45 ft | 60 mm | 75 km | 90 cm |

## Trapezoids

✏️ *Find the area of each trapezoid.*

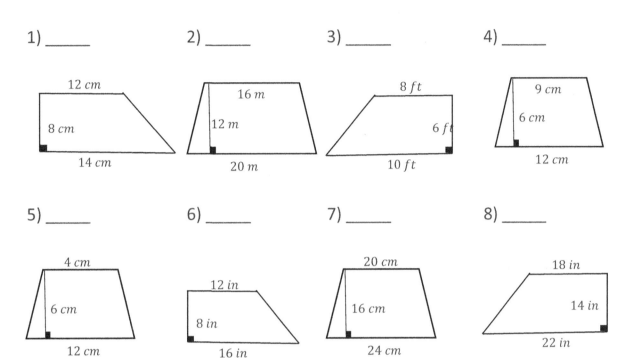

1) _____

12 cm

8 cm

14 cm

2) _____

16 m

12 m

20 m

3) _____

8 ft

6 ft

10 ft

4) _____

9 cm

6 cm

12 cm

5) _____

4 cm

6 cm

12 cm

6) _____

12 in

8 in

16 in

7) _____

20 cm

16 cm

24 cm

8) _____

18 in

14 in

22 in

✏️ *Solve.*

9) A trapezoid has an area of 78 $cm^2$ and its height is 10 $cm$ and one base is 8 $cm$. What is the other base length? _____

10) If a trapezoid has an area of 160 $ft^2$ and the lengths of the bases are 12 $ft$ and 8 $ft$, find the height. _____

11) If a trapezoid has an area of 180 $m^2$ and its height is 8 $m$ and one base is 10 $m$, find the other base length. _____

12) The area of a trapezoid is 150 $ft^2$ and its height is 20 $ft$. If one base of the trapezoid is 12 $ft$, what is the other base length? _____

# Rectangular Prisms

✎ *Find the volume of each Rectangular Prism.*

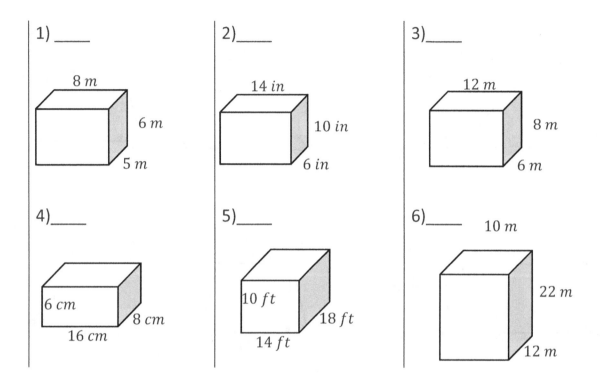

1) _____

8 m
6 m
5 m

2) _____

14 in
10 in
6 in

3) _____

12 m
8 m
6 m

4) _____

6 cm
8 cm
16 cm

5) _____

10 ft
18 ft
14 ft

6) _____

10 m
22 m
12 m

✎ *Find the surface area of each Rectangular Prism.*

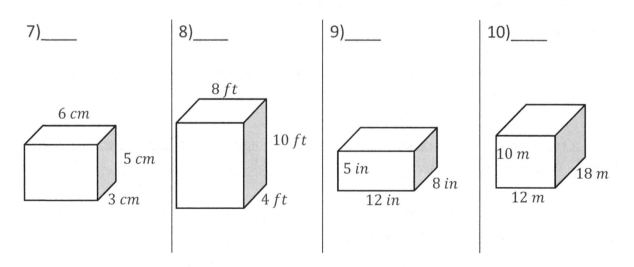

7) _____

6 cm
5 cm
3 cm

8) _____

8 ft
10 ft
4 ft

9) _____

5 in
8 in
12 in

10) _____

10 m
18 m
12 m

## Cylinder

✏️ *Find the volume of each Cylinder.* ($\pi = 3.14$)

1) _____
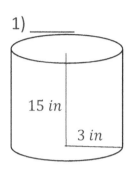
15 in
3 in

2) _____
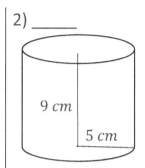
9 cm
5 cm

3) _____
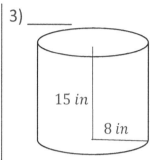
15 in
8 in

4) _____
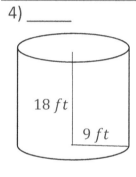
18 ft
9 ft

5) _____
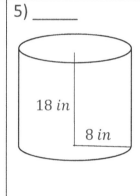
18 in
8 in

6) _____
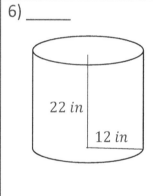
22 in
12 in

✏️ *Find the surface area of each Cylinder.* ($\pi = 3.14$)

7) _____
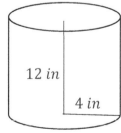
12 in
4 in

8) _____
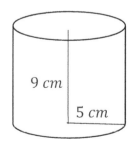
9 cm
5 cm

9) _____
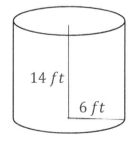
14 ft
6 ft

10) _____
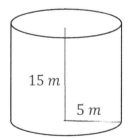
15 m
5 m

# Answers – Chapter 11

## The Pythagorean Theorem

1) *no*

2) *no*

3) *no*

4) *yes*

5) *no*

6) *no*

7) *yes*

8) *yes*

9) 25

10) 12

11) 6

12) 34

13) 10

14) 5

15) 13

16) 25

## Triangles

1) 7°

2) 55°

3) 43°

4) 55°

5) 45°

6) 46°

7) 52°

8) 71°

9) 27

10) 54

11) 72 $cm^2$

12) 72 $in^2$

## Polygons

1) 24 $cm$

2) 40 $m$

3) 40 $cm$

4) 32 $m$

5) 96 $m$

6) 56 $m$

7) 28 $cm$

8) 120 $ft$

9) 64 $ft$

10) 80 $in$

11) 60 $ft$

12) 180 $in$

## Circles

1) 37.68 in

2) 62.8 cm

3) 119.32 ft

4) 75.36 m

5) 113.04 cm

6) 94.2 miles

7) 119.32 in

8) 138.16 ft

9) 157 m

10) 175.84 m

11) 219.8 in

12) 314 ft

|          | Radius        | Diameter      | Circumference    | Area                      |
|----------|---------------|---------------|------------------|---------------------------|
| Circle 1 | 2 inches      | 4 inches      | 12.56 inches     | 12.56 square inches       |
| Circle 2 | 4 meters      | 8 meters      | 25.12 meters     | 50.24 square meters       |
| Circle 3 | 6 feet        | 12 feet       | 37.68 feet       | 113.04 square feet        |
| Circle 4 | 8 miles       | 16 miles      | 50.24 miles      | 200.96 square miles       |
| Circle 5 | 4.5 kilometers| 9 kilometers  | 28.26 kilometers | 63.585 square kilometers  |
| Circle 6 | 7 centimeters | 14 centimeters| 43.96 centimeters| 153.86 square centimeters |
| Circle 7 | 9 feet        | 18 feet       | 56.52 feet       | 254.34 square feet        |
| Circle 8 | 5 meters      | 10 meters     | 31.4 meters      | 78.5 square meters        |
| Circle 9 | 11 inches     | 22 inches     | 69.08 inches     | 379.94 square inches      |
| Circle 10| 10 feet       | 20 feet       | 62.8 feet        | 314 square feet           |

## Cubes

1) $42.875 \ cm^3$

2) $74.088 \ cm^3$

3) $614.125 \ ft^3$

4) $1,000 \ m^3$

5) $2,197 \ in^3$

6) $614.125 \ m^3$

7) $421.875 \ km^3$

8) $274.625 \ cm^3$

9) $4,096 \ ft^3$

10) $4,913 \ mm^3$

11) $27,000 \ in^3$

12) $64,000 \ km^3$

13) $3,750 \ m^2$

14) $9,600 \ m^2$

15) $12,150 \ ft^2$

16) $21,600 \ mm^2$

17) $33,750 \ km^2$

18) $48,600 \ cm^2$

**Trapezoids**

1) $104 \ cm^2$

2) $216 \ m^2$

3) $54 \ ft^2$

4) $63 \ cm^2$

5) $48 \ cm^2$

6) $112 \ in^2$

7) $352 \ cm^2$

8) $280 \ in^2$

9) $7.6 \ cm$

10) $16 \ ft$

11) $35 \ m$

12) $3 \ ft$

**Rectangular Prisms**

1) $240 \ m^3$

2) $840 \ in^3$

3) $576 \ m^3$

4) $768 \ cm^3$

5) $2,520 \ ft^3$

6) $2,640 \ m^3$

7) $126 \ cm^2$

8) $304 \ ft^2$

9) $392 \ in^2$

10) $1,032 \ m^2$

**Cylinder**

1) $423.9 \ in^3$

2) $706.5 \ cm^3$

3) $3,014.4 \ in^3$

4) $4,578.12 \ ft^3$

5) $3,617.28 \ in^3$

6) $9,947.52 \ in^3$

7) $401.92 \ in^2$

8) $439.6 \ cm^2$

9) $753.6 \ ft^2$

10) $628 \ m^2$

# Chapter 12: Statistics

**Math Topics that you'll learn in this Chapter:**

- ✓ Mean, Median, Mode, and Range of the Given Data
- ✓ Pie Graph
- ✓ Probability Problems
- ✓ Permutations and Combinations

117

# Mean, Median, Mode, and Range of the Given Data

## ✎ Find the values of the Given Data.

1) 5, 12, 2, 2, 6

    Mode: _____      Range: _____

    Mean: _____      Median: _____

2) 5, 9, 3, 6, 4, 3

    Mode: _____      Range: _____

    Mean: _____      Median: _____

3) 12, 5, 8, 7, 8

    Mode: _____      Range: _____

    Mean: _____      Median: _____

4) 9, 7, 12, 7, 3, 4

    Mode: _____      Range: _____

    Mean: _____      Median: _____

5) 9, 7, 10, 5, 7, 4, 14

    Mode: _____      Range: _____

    Mean: _____      Median: _____

6) 8, 1, 6, 6, 9, 2, 17

    Mode: _____      Range: _____

    Mean: _____      Median: _____

7) 14, 5, 2, 7, 10, 7, 8, 13

    Mode: _____      Range: _____

    Mean: _____      Median: _____

8) 12, 14, 6, 4, 10, 8, 2

    Mode: _____      Range: _____

    Mean: _____      Median: _____

9) 17, 13, 16, 12, 14, 24

    Mode: _____      Range: _____

    Mean: _____      Median: _____

10) 18, 15, 10, 8, 4, 7, 8, 18

    Mode: _____      Range: _____

    Mean: _____      Median: _____

## Pie Graph

*The circle graph below shows all Wilson's expenses for last month. Wilson spent $300 on his bills last month.*

**Answer following questions based on the Pie graph.**

Wilson's last month expenses

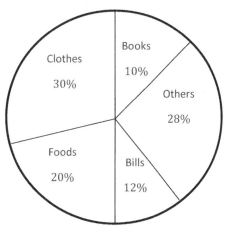

1) How much was Wilson's total expenses last month? _____

2) How much did Wilson spend on his clothes last month? _____

3) How much did Wilson spend for foods last month? _____

4) How much did Wilson spend on his books last month? _____

5) What fraction is Wilson's expenses for his bills and clothes out of his total expenses last month? _____

## Probability Problems

1) If there are 15 red balls and 30 blue balls in a basket, what is the probability that Oliver will pick out a red ball from the basket? _____

| Gender | Under 45 | 45 or older | Total |
|--------|----------|-------------|-------|
| Male | 12 | 6 | 18 |
| Female | 5 | 7 | 12 |
| Total | 17 | 13 | 30 |

2) The table above shows the distribution of age and gender for 30 employees in a company. If one employee is selected at random, what is the probability that the employee selected be either a female under age 45 or a male age 45 or older? _____

3) A number is chosen at random from 1 to 18. Find the probability of not selecting a composite number. (A composite number is a number that is divisible by itself, 1 and at least one other whole number) _____

4) There are 6 blue marbles, 8 red marbles, and 5 yellow marbles in a box. If Ava randomly selects a marble from the box, what is the probability of selecting a red or yellow marble? _____

5) A bag contains 20 balls: three green, six black, eight blue, a brown, a red and one white. If 19 balls are removed from the bag at random, what is the probability that a brown ball has been removed? _____

6) There are only red and blue marbles in a box. The probability of choosing a red marble in the box at random is one third. If there are 160 blue marbles, how many marbles are in the box? _____

# Permutations and Combinations

✍ *Calculate the value of each.*

1) $5! = \underline{\quad}$

2) $6! = \underline{\quad}$

3) $8! = \underline{\quad}$

4) $5! + 6! = \underline{\quad}$

5) $8! + 3! = \underline{\quad}$

6) $6! + 7! = \underline{\quad}$

7) $8! + 4! = \underline{\quad}$

8) $9! - 3! = \underline{\quad}$

✍ *Solve each word problems.*

9) Sophia is baking cookies. She uses milk, flour and eggs. How many different orders of ingredients can she try? \_\_\_\_\_

10) William is planning for his vacation. He wants to go to restaurant, watch a movie, go to the beach, and play basketball. How many different ways of ordering are there for him? \_\_\_\_\_

11) How many 7 −digit numbers can be named using the digits $1, 2, 3, 4, 5, 6$ and 7 without repetition? \_\_\_\_\_

12) In how many ways can 9 boys be arranged in a straight line? \_\_\_\_\_

13) In how many ways can 8 athletes be arranged in a straight line? \_\_\_\_\_

14) A professor is going to arrange her 6 students in a straight line. In how many ways can she do this? \_\_\_\_\_

15) How many code symbols can be formed with the letters for the word BLUE? \_\_\_\_\_

16) In how many ways a team of 8 basketball players can choose a captain and co-captain? \_\_\_\_\_

**Effortless Math Education**

# Answers – Chapter 12

## Mean, Median, Mode, and Range of the Given Data

1) Mode: 2     Range: 10   Mean: 5.4     Median: 5

2) Mode: 3     Range: 6    Mean: 5      Median: 4.5

3) Mode: 8     Range: 7    Mean: 8      Median: 8

4) Mode: 7     Range: 9    Mean: 7      Median: 7

5) Mode: 7     Range: 10   Mean: 8      Median: 7

6) Mode: 6     Range: 16   Mean: 7      Median: 6

7) Mode: 7     Range: 12   Mean: 8.25   Median: 7.5

8) Mode: no mode   Range: 12   Mean: 8      Median: 8

9) Mode: no mode   Range: 12   Mean: 16     Median: 15

10) Mode: 8,18    Range: 14   Mean: 11     Median: 9

## Pie Graph

1) $2,500

2) $750

3) $500

4) $250

5) $\frac{21}{50}$

## Probability Problems

1) $\frac{1}{3}$

2) $\frac{11}{30}$

3) $\frac{7}{18}$

4) $\frac{13}{19}$

5) $\frac{19}{20}$

6) 240

## Permutations and Combinations

1) 120

2) 720

3) 40,320

4) 840

5) 40,326

6) 5,760

7) 40,344

8) 362,874

9) 6

10) 24

11) 5,040

12) 362,880

13) 40,320

14) 720

15) 24

16) 56

# Chapter 13:
# Functions Operations

**Math Topics that you'll learn in this Chapter:**

- ✓ Function Notation and Evaluation
- ✓ Adding and Subtracting Functions
- ✓ Multiplying and Dividing Functions
- ✓ Composition of Functions

# Function Notation and Evaluation

✎ *Evaluate each function.*

1) $f(x) = x - 3$, find $f(-2)$

_____

2) $g(x) = x + 5$, find $g(6)$

_____

3) $h(x) = x + 8$, find $h(2)$

_____

4) $f(x) = -x - 7$, find $f(5)$

_____

5) $f(x) = 2x - 7$, find $f(-1)$

_____

6) $w(x) = -2 - 4x$, find $w(5)$

_____

7) $g(n) = 6n - 3$, find $g(-2)$

_____

8) $h(x) = -8x + 12$, find $h(3)$

_____

9) $k(n) = 14 - 3n$, find $k(3)$

_____

10) $g(x) = 4x - 4$, find $g(-2)$

_____

11) $k(n) = 8n - 7$, find $k(4)$

_____

12) $w(n) = -2n + 14$, find $w(5)$

_____

13) $h(x) = 5x - 18$, find $h(8)$

_____

14) $g(n) = 2n^2 + 2$, find $g(5)$

_____

15) $f(x) = 3x^2 - 13$, find $f(2)$

_____

16) $g(n) = 5n^2 + 7$, find $g(-3)$

_____

17) $h(n) = 5n^2 - 10$, find $h(4)$

_____

18) $g(x) = -3x^2 - 6x$, find $g(2)$

_____

19) $k(n) = 4n^3 + n$, find $k(-5)$

_____

20) $f(x) = -3x + 10$, find $f(3x)$

_____

21) $k(a) = 4a + 9$, find $k(a - 1)$

_____

22) $h(x) = 8x + 4$, find $h(5x)$

_____

# Adding and Subtracting Functions

✎ *Perform the indicated operation.*

1) $f(x) = x + 4$

   $g(x) = 2x + 5$

   Find $(f - g)(2)$

   _____

2) $g(x) = x - 2$

   $f(x) = -x - 6$

   Find $(g - f)(-2)$

   _____

3) $h(t) = 4t + 4$

   $g(t) = 3t + 2$

   Find $(h + g)(-1)$

   _____

4) $g(a) = 5a - 7$

   $f(a) = a^2 + 3$

   Find $(g + f)(2)$

   _____

5) $g(x) = 4x - 5$

   $f(x) = 6x^2 + 5$

   Find $(g - f)(-2)$

   _____

6) $h(x) = x^2 + 3$

   $g(x) = -4x + 1$

   Find $(h + g)(4)$

   _____

7) $f(x) = -3x - 9$

   $g(x) = x^2 + 5$

   Find $(f - g)(6)$

   _____

8) $h(n) = -4n^2 + 9$

   $g(n) = 5n + 6$

   Find $(h - g)(5)$

   _____

9) $g(x) = 4x^2 - 3x - 1$

   $f(x) = 6x + 10$

   Find $(g - f)(a)$

   _____

10) $g(t) = -6t - 7$

    $f(t) = -t^2 + 3t + 15$

    Find $(g + f)(t)$

    _____

## Multiplying and Dividing Functions

✐ *Perform the indicated operation.*

1) $g(x) = x + 6$

$f(x) = x + 4$

Find $(g.f)(2)$

_____

2) $f(x) = 3x$

$h(x) = -x + 5$

Find $(f.h)(-2)$

_____

3) $g(a) = a + 5$

$h(a) = 2a - 4$

Find $(g.h)(4)$

_____

4) $f(x) = 3x + 2$

$h(x) = 2x - 3$

Find $(\frac{f}{h})(2)$

_____

5) $f(x) = a^2 - 2$

$g(x) = -4 + 3a$

Find $(\frac{f}{g})(2)$

_____

6) $g(a) = 4a + 6$

$f(a) = 2a - 8$

Find $(\frac{g}{f})(3)$

_____

7) $g(t) = t^2 + 6$

$h(t) = 2t - 3$

Find $(g.h)(-3)$

_____

8) $g(x) = x^2 + 3x + 4$

$h(x) = 2x + 6$

Find $(g.h)(2)$

_____

9) $g(a) = 2a^2 - 5a + 1$

$f(a) = 2a^3 - 6$

Find $(\frac{g}{f})(4)$

_____

10) $g(x) = -3x^2 + 4 - 2x$

$f(x) = x^2 - 5$

Find $(g.f)(3)$

_____

# Composition of Functions

✎ **Using $f(x) = x + 6$ and $g(x) = 3x$, find:**

1) $f\big(g(1)\big) =$ ____

2) $f\big(g(-1)\big) =$ ____

3) $g\big(f(-3)\big) =$ ____

4) $g\big(f(4)\big) =$ ____

5) $f\big(g(2)\big) =$ ____

6) $g\big(f(3)\big) =$ ____

✎ **Using $f(x) = 2x + 5$ and $g(x) = x - 2$, find:**

7) $g\big(f(2)\big) =$ ____

8) $g\big(f(-2)\big) =$ ____

9) $f\big(g(5)\big) =$ ____

10) $f\big(f(4)\big) =$ ____

11) $g\big(f(3)\big) =$ ____

12) $g\big(f(-3)\big) =$ ____

✎ **Using $f(x) = 4x - 2$ and $g(x) = x - 5$, find:**

13) $g\big(f(-2)\big) =$ ____

14) $f\big(f(4)\big) =$ ____

15) $f\big(g(5)\big) =$ ____

16) $f\big(f(3)\big) =$ ____

17) $g\big(f(-3)\big) =$ ____

18) $g\big(g(6)\big) =$ ____

✎ **Using $f(x) = 6x + 2$ and $g(x) = 2x - 3$, find:**

19) $f\big(g(-3)\big) =$ ____

20) $g\big(f(5)\big) =$ ____

21) $f\big(g(4)\big) =$ ____

22) $f\big(f(3)\big) =$ ____

**Effortless Math Education**

# Answers – Chapter 13

## Function Notation and Evaluation

1) $-5$

2) $11$

3) $10$

4) $-12$

5) $-9$

6) $-22$

7) $-15$

8) $-12$

9) $5$

10) $-12$

11) $25$

12) $4$

13) $22$

14) $52$

15) $-1$

16) $52$

17) $70$

18) $-24$

19) $-505$

20) $-9x + 10$

21) $4a + 5$

22) $40x + 4$

## Adding and Subtracting Functions

1) $-3$

2) $0$

3) $-1$

4) $10$

5) $-42$

6) $4$

7) $-68$

8) $-122$

9) $4a^2 - 9a - 11$

10) $-t^2 - 3t + 8$

## Multiplying and Dividing Functions

1) $48$

2) $-42$

3) $36$

4) $8$

5) $1$

6) $-9$

7) $-135$

8) $140$

9) $\dfrac{13}{122}$

10) $-116$

## Composition of Functions

1) $f\big(g(1)\big) = 9$

2) $f\big(g(-1)\big) = 3$

3) $g\big(f(-3)\big) = 9$

4) $g\big(f(4)\big) = 30$

5) $f\big(g(2)\big) = 12$

6) $g\big(f(3)\big) = 27$

7) $g\big(f(2)\big) = 7$

8) $g\big(f(-2)\big) = -1$

9) $f\big(g(5)\big) = 11$

10) $f\big(f(4)\big) = 31$

11) $g\big(f(3)\big) = 9$

12) $g\big(f(-3)\big) = -3$

13) $g\big(f(-2)\big) = -15$

14) $f\big(f(4)\big) = 54$

15) $f\big(g(5)\big) = -2$

16) $f\big(f(3)\big) = 38$

17) $g\big(f(-3)\big) = -19$

18) $g\big(g(6)\big) = -4$

19) $f\big(g(-3)\big) = -52$

20) $g\big(f(5)\big) = 61$

21) $f\big(g(4)\big) = 32$

22) $f\big(f(3)\big) = 122$

# Time to Test

## Time to refine your skill with a practice examination.

Take a practice GED Math Test to simulate the test day experience. After you've finished, score your test using the answer key.

## Before You Start

- You'll need a pencil and a calculator to take the test.

- There are two types of questions:

Multiple choice questions: for each of these questions, there are four or more

possible answers. Choose which one is best.

Grid-ins questions: for these questions, write your answer in the box provided.

- It's okay to guess. You won't lose any points if you're wrong.

- The GED® Mathematical Reasoning test contains a formula sheet, which

  displays formulas relating to geometric measurement and certain algebra

  concepts. Formulas are provided to test- takers so that they may focus on

  application, rather than the memorization, of formulas.

- After you've finished the test, review the answer key to see where you

  went wrong and what areas you need to improve.

**Good luck**

# GED Mathematical Reasoning Practice Test 1

## 2024

### Two Parts

**Total number of questions:** 46

**Part 1 (Non-Calculator):** 5 questions

**Part 2 (Calculator):** 41 questions

**Total time for two parts:** 115 Minutes

133

# *GED Test Mathematics Formula Sheet*

**Area of a:**

Parallelogram

$$A = bh$$

Trapezoid

$$A = \frac{1}{2}h(b_1 + b_2)$$

**Surface Area and Volume of a:**

Rectangular/Right Prism

$$SA = ph + 2B \qquad V = Bh$$

Cylinder

$$SA = 2\pi rh + 2\pi r^2 \qquad V = \pi r^2 h$$

Pyramid

$$SA = \frac{1}{2}ps + B \qquad V = \frac{1}{3}Bh$$

Cone

$$SA = \pi r + \pi r^2 \qquad V = \frac{1}{3}\pi r^2 h$$

Sphere

$$SA = 4\pi r^2 \qquad V = \frac{4}{3}\pi r^3$$

($p$ = perimeter of base $B$; $\pi = 3.14$)

**Algebra**

Slope of a line

$$m = \frac{y_2 - y_1}{x_2 - x_1}$$

Slope-intercept form of the equation of a line

$$y = mx + b$$

Point-slope form of the Equation of a line

$$y - y_1 = m(x - x_1)$$

Standard form of a Quadratic equation

$$y = ax^2 + bx + c$$

Quadratic formula

$$x = \frac{-b \pm \sqrt{b^2 - 4ac}}{2a}$$

Pythagorean theorem

$$a^2 + b^2 = c^2$$

Simple interest

$$I = prt$$

($I$ = interest, $p$ = principal, $r$ = rate, $t$ = time)

# GED Mathematical Reasoning Practice Test 1

## Part 1 (Non-Calculator)

**5 questions**

**Total time for two parts (Non-Calculator, and Calculator parts):** 115 Minutes

**You may NOT use a calculator on this part.**

135

1) The surface area of a cylinder is $150\pi\ cm^2$. If its height is $10\ cm$, what is the radius of the cylinder?

   ☐A. $13\ cm$                      ☐B. $11\ cm$

   ☐C. $15\ cm$                      ☐D. $5\ cm$

2) A tree 32 feet tall casts a shadow 12 feet long. Jack is 6 feet tall. How long is Jack's shadow?

   ☐A. $2.25\ ft$                    ☐B. $4\ ft$

   ☐C. $4.25\ ft$                    ☐D. $8\ ft$

3) What is the product of all possible values of $x$ in the following equation?

$$|2x - 6| = 12$$

   ☐A. $-27$                        ☐B. $-3$

   ☐C. $9$                           ☐D. $27$

4) What is the slope of a line that is perpendicular to the line $3x - y = 6$?

   ☐A. $-3$                        ☐B. $-\frac{1}{3}$

   ☐C. $2$                           ☐D. $6$

5) What is the value of the expression $3(x - 2y) + (2 - x)^2$ when $x = 5$ and $y = -3$ ?

   ☐A. $-22$                        ☐B. $24$

   ☐C. $42$                          ☐D. $88$

# GED Mathematical Reasoning Practice Test 1

## Part 2 (Calculator)

**41 questions**

**Total time for two parts (Non-Calculator, and Calculator parts):** 115 Minutes

**You may use a calculator on this part.**

137

6) If $x - 4(x + 2) = -15.5$, what is the value of $x$?
Write your answer in the box below.

☐

7) Which of the following answers represents the compound inequality?
$$-4 \leq 4x - 8 < 16?$$

☐A. $-2 \leq x \leq 8$        ☐B. $-2 < x \leq 8$

☐C. $1 < x \leq 6$        ☐D. $1 \leq x < 6$

8) What is the volume of a box with the following dimensions?
High = 4 $cm$      width = 5 $cm$      length = 6 $cm$

☐A. $15\ cm^3$        ☐B. $60\ cm^3$

☐C. $90\ cm^3$        ☐D. $120\ cm^3$

9) Simplify the expression.

$$(6x^3 - 8x^2 + 2x^4) - (4x^2 - 2x^4 + 2x^3)$$

☐A. $4x^4 + 4x^3 - 12x^2$        ☐B. $4x^3 - 12x^2$

☐C. $4x^4 + 4x^3 + 12x^2$        ☐D. $8x^3 - 12x^2$

10) In two successive years, the population of a town is increased by 15% and 20%. What percent of the population is increased after two years?

☐A. 32%        ☐B. 35%

☐C. 38%        ☐D. 68%

11) Last week 24,000 fans attended a football match. This week three times as many bought tickets, but one sixth of them cancelled their tickets. How many are attending this week?

☐A. 48,000        ☐B. 54,000

☐C. 60,000        ☐D. 72,000

12) What is the perimeter of a square in centimeters that has an area of $595.36\ cm^2$?

Write your answer in the box below. (don't write the measurement)

☐

13) Which of the following shows the numbers from least to greatest?

$$\frac{2}{3}, 0.68, 67\%, \frac{4}{5}$$

☐A. $67\%, 0.68, \frac{2}{3}, \frac{4}{5}$      ☐B. $67\%, 0.68, \frac{4}{5}, \frac{2}{3}$

☐C. $0.68, 67\%, \frac{2}{3}, \frac{4}{5}$      ☐D. $\frac{2}{3}, 67\%, 0.68, \frac{4}{5}$

14) The mean of 50 test scores was calculated as 88. But it turned out that one of the scores was misread as 94 but it was 69. What is the correct mean of the test scores?

☐A. 85      ☐B. 87

☐C. 87.5      ☐D. 88.5

15) Two dice are thrown simultaneously, what is the probability of getting a sum of 5 or 8?

☐A. $\frac{1}{3}$      ☐B. $\frac{1}{4}$

☐C. $\frac{1}{16}$      ☐D. $\frac{11}{36}$

16) A swimming pool holds 2,000 cubic feet of water. The swimming pool is 25 feet long and 10 feet wide. How deep is the swimming pool?

Write your answer in the box below. (don't write the measurement)

17) Mr. Carlos family are choosing a menu for their reception. They have 3 choices of appetizers, 5 choices of entrees, 4 choices of cake. How many different menu combinations are possible for them to choose?

☐A. 12      ☐B. 32

☐C. 60      ☐D. 120

18) In a stadium the ratio of home fans to visiting fans in a crowd is $5 : 7$. Which of the following could be the total number of fans in the stadium? (Select one or more answer choices)

☐A. 12,324      ☐B. 16,788

☐C. 42,326      ☐D. 44,566

☐E. 66,812

19) What is the area of a square whose diagonal is 8?

   ☐A. 16                 ☐B. 32

   ☐C. 36                 ☐D. 64

20) Anita's trick–or–treat bag contains 12 pieces of chocolate, 18 suckers, 18 pieces of gum, 24 pieces of licorice. If she randomly pulls a piece of candy from her bag, what is the probability of her pulling out a piece of sucker?

   ☐A. $\frac{1}{3}$               ☐B. $\frac{1}{4}$

   ☐C. $\frac{1}{6}$               ☐D. $\frac{1}{12}$

21) Which of the following points lies on the line $x + 2y = 4$? (Select one or more answer choices)

   ☐A. $(-2, 3)$          ☐B. $(1, 2)$

   ☐C. $(-1, 3)$          ☐D. $(-3, 4)$

   ☐E. $(0, 2)$

22) The perimeter of a rectangular yard is 60 meters. What is its length if its width is twice its length?

   ☐A. 10 meters         ☐B. 18 meters

   ☐C. 20 meters         ☐D. 24 meters

23) The average of 6 numbers is 12. The average of 4 of those numbers is 10. What is the average of the other two numbers?

   ☐A. 10                 ☐B. 12

   ☐C. 14                 ☐D. 16

24) What is the value of $x$ in the following system of equations?

$$2x + 5y = 11$$
$$4x - 2y = -14$$

   ☐A. $-1$              ☐B. 1

   ☐C. $-2$              ☐D. 4

25) The perimeter of the trapezoid below is $36\ cm$. What is its area?

   ☐A. $26\ cm^2$         ☐B. $70\ cm^2$

   ☐C. $48\ cm^2$         ☐D. $24\ cm^2$

12 cm

6 cm                8 cm

26) A card is drawn at random from a standard 52–card deck, what is the probability that the card is of Hearts? (The deck includes 13 of each suit clubs, diamonds, hearts, and spades)

☐A. $\frac{1}{3}$                  ☐B. $\frac{1}{4}$

☐C. $\frac{1}{6}$                  ☐D. $\frac{1}{52}$

27) The average of five numbers is 25. If a sixth number that is greater than 42 is added, then, which of the following could be the new average? (Select one or more answer choices)

☐A. 25                  ☐B. 26

☐C. 27                  ☐D. 28

☐E. 42

28) The diagonal of a rectangle is 10 inches long and the height of the rectangle is 8 inches. What is the perimeter of the rectangle in inches?

Write your answer in the box below.

```
┌─────────────────────────┐
│                         │
│                         │
└─────────────────────────┘
```

29) The ratio of boys and girls in a class is 4: 7. If there are 44 students in the class, how many more boys should be enrolled to make the ratio 1: 1?

☐A. 8                  ☐B. 10

☐C. 12                  ☐D. 14

30) Mr. Jones saves $2,500 out of his monthly family income of $55,000. What fractional part of his income does he save?

☐A. $\frac{1}{22}$                  ☐B. $\frac{1}{11}$

☐C. $\frac{3}{25}$                  ☐D. $\frac{2}{15}$

31) Jason needs an 75% average in his writing class to pass. On his first 4 exams, he earned scores of 68%, 72%, 85%, and 90%. What is the minimum score Jason can earn on his fifth and final test to pass?

Write your answer in the box below.

```
┌─────────────────────────┐
│                         │
│                         │
└─────────────────────────┘
```

32) What is the value of $x$ in the following equation? $\frac{2}{3}x + \frac{1}{6} = \frac{1}{3}$

☐A. 6                          ☐B. $\frac{1}{2}$

☐C. $\frac{1}{3}$                          ☐D. $\frac{1}{4}$

33) A bank is offering 3.5% simple interest on a savings account. If you deposit $12,000, how much interest will you earn in two years?

☐A. $420                      ☐B. $840

☐C. $4200                     ☐D. $8,400

34) Simplify $6x^2y^3(2x^2y)^3 =$

☐A. $12x^4y^6$                  ☐B. $12x^8y^6$

☐C. $48x^4y^6$                  ☐D. $48x^8y^6$

35) What is the surface area of the cylinder below?

☐A. $48\pi\ in^2$

☐B. $57\pi\ in^2$

☐C. $66\pi\ in^2$

☐D. $288\pi\ in^2$

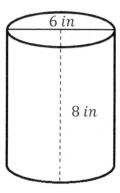
6 in

8 in

36) The square of a number is $\frac{25}{64}$. What is the cube of that number?

☐A. $\frac{5}{8}$                          ☐B. $\frac{25}{254}$

☐C. $\frac{125}{512}$                        ☐D. $\frac{125}{64}$

37) What is the median of these numbers? $2, 27, 28, 19, 67, 44, 35$

☐A. 19                          ☐B. 28

☐C. 44                          ☐D. 35

38) A cruise line ship left Port A and traveled 80 miles due west and then 150 miles due north. At this point, what is the shortest distance from the cruise to port A in miles?

Write your answer in the box below.

39) What is the equivalent temperature of $104°F$ in Celsius? $C = \frac{5}{9}(F - 32)$

☐A. 32            ☐B. 40

☐C. 48            ☐D. 52

40) If 40% of a number is 4, what is the number?

☐A. 4            ☐B. 8

☐C. 10            ☐D. 12

41) The circle graph below shows all Mr. Green's expenses for last month. If he spent $660 on his car, how much did he spend for his rent?

☐A. $700

☐B. $740

☐C. $780

☐D. $810

Mr. Green's monthly expenses

Bills 13%

Rent 27%

Others 28%

Car 22%

Foods 10%

42) Jason is 9 miles ahead of Joe running at 5.5 miles per hour and Joe is running at the speed of 7 miles per hour. How long does it take Joe to catch Jason?

☐A. 3 *hours*            ☐B. 4 *hours*

☐C. 6 *hours*            ☐D. 8 *hours*

43) 55 students took an exam and 11 of them failed. What percent of the students passed the exam?

☐A. 20%            ☐B. 40%

☐C. 60%            ☐D. 80%

44) If 150% of a number is 75, then what is the 90% of that number?

☐A. 45            ☐B. 50

☐C. 70            ☐D.85

45) What is the slope of the line? $4x - 2y = 6$

Write your answer in the box below.

46) A football team had $20,000 to spend on supplies. The team spent $14,000 on new balls. New sport shoes cost $120 each. Which of the following inequalities represent the number of new shoes the team can purchase?

☐A. $120x + 14,000 \leq 20,000$   ☐B. $120x + 14,000 \geq 20,000$

☐C. $14,000x + 120 \leq 20,000$   ☐D. $14,000x + 120 \geq 20,000$

**End of GED Mathematical Reasoning Practice Test 1.**

# GED Mathematical Reasoning Practice Test 2

## 2024

### Two Parts

**Total number of questions:** 46

**Part 1 (Non-Calculator):** 5 questions

**Part 2 (Calculator):** 41 questions

**Total time for two parts:** 115 Minutes

145

# *GED Test Mathematics Formula Sheet*

**Area of a:**

Parallelogram

$$A = bh$$

Trapezoid

$$A = \frac{1}{2}h(b_1 + b_2)$$

**Surface Area and Volume of a:**

Rectangular/Right Prism

$$SA = ph + 2B \qquad V = Bh$$

Cylinder

$$SA = 2\pi rh + 2\pi r^2 \qquad V = \pi r^2 h$$

Pyramid

$$SA = \frac{1}{2}ps + B \qquad V = \frac{1}{3}Bh$$

Cone

$$SA = \pi r + \pi r^2 \qquad V = \frac{1}{3}\pi r^2 h$$

Sphere

$$SA = 4\pi r^2 \qquad V = \frac{4}{3}\pi r^3$$

($p$ = perimeter of base $B$; $\pi = 3.14$)

**Algebra**

Slope of a line

$$m = \frac{y_2 - y_1}{x_2 - x_1}$$

Slope-intercept form of the equation of a line

$$y = mx + b$$

Point-slope form of the Equation of a line

$$y - y_1 = m(x - x_1)$$

Standard form of a Quadratic equation

$$y = ax^2 + bx + c$$

Quadratic formula

$$x = \frac{-b \pm \sqrt{b^2 - 4ac}}{2a}$$

Pythagorean theorem

$$a^2 + b^2 = c^2$$

Simple interest

$$I = prt$$

($I$ = interest, $p$ = principal, $r$ = rate, $t$ = time)

# GED Mathematical Reasoning Practice Test 2

## Part 1 (Non-Calculator)

**5 questions**

**Total time for two parts (Non-Calculator, and Calculator parts):** 115 Minutes

**You may NOT use a calculator on this part.**

147

1) If $n$ is an even integer that is less than $-3.34$, what is the greatest possible value of $n$?

   ☐A. $-1$                         ☐B. $-2$

   ☐C. $-4$                        ☐D. $-5$

2) What is the area of an isosceles right triangle that has one leg that measures $8\ cm$?

   ☐A. $6\ cm^2$                   ☐B. $12\ cm^2$

   ☐C. $18\ cm^2$                ☐D. $32\ cm^2$

3) In the figure below, a square is inscribed in a circle. Calculate the shaded area in the figure below. Knowing that the radius of the circle is $6\ cm$. ($\pi = 3.14$)

   ☐A. $73.65\ cm^2$

   ☐B. $69.90\ cm^2$

   ☐C. $72.69\ cm^2$

   ☐D. $88.04\ cm^2$

4) How many different two-digit numbers can be formed from the digits $6, 7$, and $5$, if the numbers must be even and no digit can be repeated?

   ☐A. $1$                            ☐B. $2$

   ☐C. $3$                            ☐D. $4$

5) If $360\ kg$ of vegetables is packed in $90$ boxes, how much vegetables will each box contain?

   ☐A. $2.5\ kg$                  ☐B. $3\ kg$

   ☐C. $4\ kg$                     ☐D. $6.5\ kg$

# GED Mathematical Reasoning Practice Test 2

## Part 2 (Calculator)

**41 questions**

**Total time for two parts (Non-Calculator, and Calculator parts):** 115 Minutes

**You may use a calculator on this part.**

6) $\frac{5}{8}$ of a number is 90. Find the number.

Write your answer in the box below.

7) In the figure below, $LMNO$ and $JMPQ$ are squares. Point $O$ is the center of the circle, and points $L$ and $N$ are on the circle. If the area of the square is 16 square centimeters, what is the area, in square centimeters, of the shaded part? $(\pi = 3.14)$

Write your answer in the box below.

8) The set of possible values of $n$ is $\{5, 3, 7\}$. What is the set of possible values of $m$ if $2m = n + 5$?

☐A. $\{2, 4, 7\}$       ☐B. $\{5, 4, 6\}$

☐C. $\{3, 2, 5\}$       ☐D. $\{4, 5, 8\}$

9) The following table represents the value of $x$ and function $f(x)$. Which of the following could be the equation of the function $f(x)$?

☐A. $f(x) = x^2 - 5$

☐B. $f(x) = x^2 - 1$

☐C. $f(x) = \sqrt{x + 2}$

☐D. $f(x) = \sqrt{x} + 4$

| $x$ | $f(x)$ |
|-----|--------|
| 1 | 5 |
| 4 | 6 |
| 9 | 7 |
| 16 | 8 |

10) Jack scored a mean of 80 per test in his first 4 tests. In his $5^{th}$ test, he scored 90. What was Jack's mean score for the 5 tests?

☐A. 70       ☐B. 75

☐C. 80       ☐D. 82

11) If $0.00104 = \dfrac{104}{x}$, what is the value of $x$?

    ☐A. 1,000                 ☐B. 10,000

    ☐C. 100,000             ☐D. 1,000,000

12) What is the value of $x$ in the figure below?

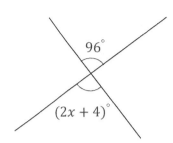

    ☐A. $32°$

    ☐B. $46°$

    ☐C. $54°$

    ☐D. $63°$

13) What is the value of the following expression? $|-5| + 9 \times 2\frac{1}{3} + (-3)^2 =$

    ☐A. 26                   ☐B. 35

    ☐C. 43                   ☐D. 51

14) If $\dfrac{2y}{x} - \dfrac{y}{3x} = \dfrac{(…)}{3x}$ and $x \neq 0$, what expression is represented by $(…)$ ?

    ☐A. $2y + 426$           ☐B. $3y - 6$

    ☐C. $5y$                 ☐D. $6y$

15) Each number in a sequence is 4 more than twice the number that comes just before it. If 84 is a number in the sequence, what number comes just before it?

    ☐A. 26                   ☐B. 35

    ☐C. 40                   ☐D. 52

16) If $m = 6$ and $n = -3$, what is the value of $\dfrac{5 - 9(3+n)}{3m - 5(2-n)} = ?$

    ☐A. $-\dfrac{4}{7}$             ☐B. $-\dfrac{5}{7}$

    ☐C. $\dfrac{3}{7}$              ☐D. $\dfrac{2}{7}$

17) The shaded sector of the circle shown below has an area of $12\pi$ square feet. What is the circumference of the circle?

    ☐A. $24\pi \; feet$

    ☐B. $81\pi \; feet$

    ☐C. $124\pi \; feet$

    ☐D. $180\pi \; feet$

18) Which of the following is a factor of 45?

☐A. 7               ☐B. 9

☐C. 11              ☐D. 13

19) How many possible outfit combinations come from six shirts, three slacks, and six ties?

Write your answer in the box below.

20) In the following shape, the area of the circle is $16\pi$. What is the area of the square?

Write your answer in the box below.

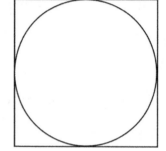

21) How many integers are between $\frac{7}{2}$ and $\frac{30}{4}$?

☐A. 3               ☐B. 4

☐C. 6               ☐D. 10

22) Triangle $ABC$ is graphed on a coordinate grid with vertices at $A\,(-3,-2)$, $B\,(-1,4)$ and $C\,(7,9)$. Triangle $ABC$ is reflected over $x$ axes to create triangle $A'\,B'\,C'$. Which order pair represents the coordinate of $C'$?

☐A. $(7,9)$         ☐B. $(-7,-9)$

☐C. $(-7,9)$        ☐D. $(7,-9)$

23) Which of the following is the solution of the following inequality?

$$2x + 4 > 11x - 12.5 - 3.5x$$

☐A. $x < 3$         ☐B. $x > 3$

☐C. $x \leq 4$      ☐D. $x \geq 4$

24) What is the volume of the following triangular prism?

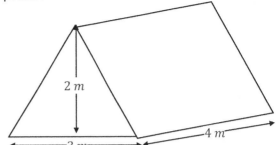

☐A. $12 \ m^3$

☐B. $24 \ m^3$

☐C. $30 \ m^3$

☐D. $32 \ m^3$

25) A student made a list of all possible products of 2 different numbers in the set below. What fraction of the products are odd?

$$\{1, 4, 6, 5, 7\}$$

☐A. $\frac{2}{5}$          ☐B. $\frac{3}{10}$

☐C. $\frac{4}{15}$          ☐D. $\frac{8}{17}$

26) Which of the following equations has a graph that is a straight line?

☐A. $y = 3x^2 + 9$          ☐B. $x^2 + y^2 = 1$

☐C. $4x - 2y = 2x$          ☐D. $7x + 2xy = 6$

27) If $5n$ is a positive even number, how many odd numbers are in the range from $5n$ up to and including $5n + 6$?

☐A. 2          ☐B. 3

☐C. 4          ☐D. 5

28) A certain insect has a mass of 85 milligrams. What is the insect's mass in grams?

☐A. 0.08          ☐B. 0.085

☐C. 0.85          ☐D. 85

29) If $2x - 5y = 10$, what is $x$ in terms of $y$?

☐A. $x = \frac{5}{2}y + 5$          ☐B. $x = \frac{2}{5}y + 10$

☐C. $x = -\frac{5}{2}y - 5$          ☐D. $x = -\frac{5}{2}y + 5$

30) Which of the following could be the product of two consecutive prime numbers? (Select one or more answer choices)

☐A. 2          ☐B. 10

☐C. 14          ☐D. 15

☐E. 35

31) Which percentage is closest in value to 0.0099?

　　☐A. 2%　　　　　　　　　　☐B. 0.1%

　　☐C. 1%　　　　　　　　　　☐D. 100%

32) When asked a certain question in a poll, 76% of the people polled answered yes. If 66 people did not answer yes to that question, what is the total number of people who were polled?

　　☐A. 75　　　　　　　　　　☐B. 156

　　☐C. 245　　　　　　　　　　☐D. 275

33) What is the average of the circumference of figure $A$ and the area of figure $B$? $(\pi = 3)$

Write your answer in the box below.

Figure $A$　　　　Figure $B$

34) The diameter of the given semi—circular slice is $18\ cm$. What is the perimeter of the slice? $(\pi = 3.14)$

Write your answer in the box below.

35) A child grows $1\frac{1}{7}$ inches in $\frac{1}{5}$ of a year. What would be his yearly growth rate in inches per year?

　　☐A. $5\frac{7}{5}$　　　　　　　　　　☐B. $5\frac{5}{7}$

　　☐C. $\frac{35}{8}$　　　　　　　　　　☐D. $\frac{2}{3}$

36) In a scale diagram, 0.15 inch represents 150 feet. How many inches represent 2.5 feet?

　　☐A. $0.001\ in$　　　　　　　　　　☐B. $0.0025\ in$

　　☐C. $0.012\ in$　　　　　　　　　　☐D. $0.002\ in$

37) If $\frac{3}{7}$ of $Z$ is 54, what is $\frac{2}{5}$ of $Z$?

　　☐A. 44.2　　　　　　　　　　☐B. 46.3

　　☐C. 48.4　　　　　　　　　　☐D. 50.4

38) If Sam spent $60 on sweets and he spent 25% of the selling price for the tip, how much did he spend?

☐A. $66  ☐B. $69

☐C. $72  ☐D. $75

39) Which of the following numbers has factors that include the smallest factor (other than 1) of 95?

☐A. 28  ☐B. 32

☐C. 39  ☐D. 45

40) $\dfrac{4^2+3^2+(-5)^2}{(9+10-11)^2}=?$

☐A. $\dfrac{25}{32}$  ☐B. 56

☐C. $-56$  ☐D. $-\dfrac{25}{32}$

41) Angle $A$ and angle $B$ are supplementary. The measure of angle $A$ is 2 times the measure of angle $B$. What is the measure of angle $A$ in degrees?

☐A. 100°  ☐B. 120°

☐C. 140°  ☐D. 160°

42) What is the value of the following expression? $3\frac{1}{4}+2\frac{4}{16}+1\frac{3}{8}+5\frac{1}{2}$

☐A. $3\frac{10}{14}$  ☐B. $4\frac{1}{2}$

☐C. $12\frac{4}{16}$  ☐D. $12\frac{3}{8}$

43) How many hours or minutes are there in 9,000 seconds? (Select one or more answer choices)

☐A. 3 hours  ☐B. 150 minutes

☐C. 1.5 hours  ☐D. 160 minuts

☐E. 2.5 hours

44) If $2y+6<30$, then $y$ could be equal to? (Select one or more answer choices)

☐A. 15  ☐B. 14

☐C. 12  ☐D. 8

☐E. $-12$

45) The least of 8 consecutive integers is $m$, and the greatest is $n$. What is the value of $\frac{m+n}{3}$ in terms of $m$?

☐A. $m + 1$ ☐B. $2m + 8$

☐C. $\frac{2m+7}{3}$ ☐D. $\frac{2m}{7}$

46) The arrow starts on space $O$ and moves clockwise around the circle. It moves through one space each minute. What space will the arrow point to in 140 minutes?

☐A. $O$

☐B. $P$

☐C. $Q$

☐D. $R$

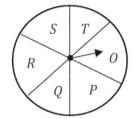

## End of GED Mathematical Reasoning Practice Test 2.

# GED Math Practice Tests Answer Keys

Now, it's time to review your results to see where you went wrong and what areas you need to improve.

| GED Math Practice Test 1 | | | | | | GED Math Practice Test 2 | | | | | |
|---|---|---|---|---|---|---|---|---|---|---|---|
| 1 | D | 21 | A, E | 41 | D | 1 | C | 21 | B | 41 | B |
| 2 | A | 22 | A | 42 | C | 2 | D | 22 | D | 42 | D |
| 3 | A | 23 | D | 43 | D | 3 | D | 23 | A | 43 | B, E |
| 4 | B | 24 | C | 44 | A | 4 | B | 24 | A | 44 | D, E |
| 5 | C | 25 | B | 45 | 2 | 5 | C | 25 | B | 45 | C |
| 6 | 2.5 | 26 | B | 46 | A | 6 | 144 | 26 | C | 46 | C |
| 7 | D | 27 | D, E | | | 7 | 3.44 | 27 | B | | |
| 8 | D | 28 | 28 | | | 8 | B | 28 | B | | |
| 9 | A | 29 | C | | | 9 | D | 29 | A | | |
| 10 | C | 30 | A | | | 10 | D | 30 | D, E | | |
| 11 | C | 31 | 60 | | | 11 | C | 31 | B | | |
| 12 | 97.6 | 32 | D | | | 12 | B | 32 | D | | |
| 13 | D | 33 | B | | | 13 | B | 33 | 45 | | |
| 14 | C | 34 | D | | | 14 | C | 34 | 46.26 | | |
| 15 | B | 35 | C | | | 15 | C | 35 | B | | |
| 16 | 8 | 36 | C | | | 16 | B | 36 | B | | |
| 17 | C | 37 | B | | | 17 | A | 37 | D | | |
| 18 | C, E | 38 | 170 | | | 18 | B | 38 | D | | |
| 19 | B | 39 | B | | | 19 | 108 | 39 | D | | |
| 20 | B | 40 | C | | | 20 | 64 | 40 | A | | |

# How to score your test

Each GED area test is scored on a scale of 100 - 200 points. To pass the GED, you must earn at least 145 on each of the four subject tests, for a total of at least 580 points (out of a possible 800).

Each subject test should be passed individually. It means that you must get 145 on each section of the test. If you failed one subject test but did well enough on another to get a total score of 580, that's still not a passing score.

There are four possible scores that you can receive on the GED Test:

**Not Passing:** This indicates that your score is lower than 145 on any of the four tests. If you do not pass, you can reschedule up to two times a year to retake any or all subjects of the GED test.

**Passing Score/High School Equivalency:** This score indicates that your score is between 145-164. Remember that points on one subject of the test do not carry over to the other subjects.

**College Ready:** This indicates that your score is between 165-175, demonstrating career and college readiness. A College Ready score shows that you may not need placement testing or remediation before beginning a college degree program.

**College Ready + Credit:** This indicates that your score is 175 or higher. This shows that you've already mastered some skills that would be taught in college courses. Depending on a school's policy, this can translate to some college credits—saving you time and money during your college education.

There are approximately 46 questions on GED Mathematical Reasoning. Similar to other subject areas, you will need a minimum score of 145 to pass the Mathematical Reasoning Test. There are 49 raw score points on the GED math test. The raw points correspond with correct answers. Most questions have one answer; therefore, they only have one point. There is more than one point for questions that have more than one answer. You'll get a raw score out of the 49 possible points. This will then be converted into your scaled score out of 200. Approximately, you need to get 32 out of 49 raw score to pass the Mathematical Reasoning section.

To score your GED Mathematical Reasoning practice tests, first find your raw score.

There were 46 questions on each GED Mathematical Reasoning practice test. All questions have one point except following questions that have 2 points:

**GED Mathematical Reasoning practice test 1:**

Question 18: Two points

Question 21: Two points

Question 27: Two points

**GED Mathematical Reasoning practice test 2:**

Question 30: Two points

Question 43: Two points

Question 44: Two points

Use the following table to convert GED Mathematical Reasoning raw score to scaled score.

| GED Mathematical Reasoning raw score to scaled score | |
|---|---|
| Raw Scores | Scaled Scores |
| *Below* 32 *(not passing)* | *Below* 145 |
| 32 − 36 | 145 − 164 |
| 37 − 40 | 165 − 175 |
| *Above* 40 | *Above* 175 |

# GED Mathematical Reasoning Practice Tests Answers and Explanations

# Mathematical Reasoning Practice Test 1

## Answers and Explanations

1) **Choice D is correct**

Formula for the Surface area of a cylinder is:

$$SA = 2\pi r^2 + 2\pi rh \rightarrow 150\pi = 2\pi r^2 + 2\pi r(10) \rightarrow r^2 + 10r - 75 = 0$$

Factor the expression and solve:

$$r^2 + 10r - 75 = 0 \rightarrow (r + 15)(r - 5) = 0 \rightarrow r = 5 \; or \; r = -15 \; (unacceptable)$$

2) **Choice A is correct**

Write a proportion and solve for the missing number. $\frac{32}{12} = \frac{6}{x} \rightarrow 32x = 6 \times 12 \rightarrow$

$$32x = 72 \rightarrow x = \frac{72}{32} = 2.25$$

3) **Choice A is correct**

To solve absolute values equations, write two equations. $2x - 6$ can equal positive $12$ or negative $12$. Therefore, $2x - 6 = 12 \Rightarrow 2x = 18 \Rightarrow x = 9$.

$$2x - 6 = -12 \Rightarrow 2x = -12 + 6 \Rightarrow 2x = -6 \Rightarrow x = -3.$$

Find the product of solutions: $-3 \times 9 = -27$

4) **Choice B is correct**

The equation of a line in slope intercept form is: $y = mx + b$. Solve for $y$. $3x - y = 6 \rightarrow$

$-y = -3x + 6$. Divide both sides by $(-1)$. Then: $-y = -3x + 6 \rightarrow y = 3x - 6$

The slope of this line is $3$. The product of the slopes of two perpendicular lines is $-1$. Therefore,

the slope of a line that is perpendicular to this line is:

$$m_1 \times m_2 = -1 \Rightarrow 3 \times m_2 = -1 \Rightarrow m_2 = \frac{-1}{3} = -\frac{1}{3}$$

**5) Choice C is correct**

Plug in the value of $x$ and $y$. $3(x - 2y) + (2 - x)^2$ when $x = 5$ and $y = -3 \rightarrow$

$3(x - 2y) + (2 - x)^2 = 3(5 - 2(-3)) + (2 - 5)^2 = 3(5 + 6) + (-3)^2 = 33 + 9 = 42$

**6) The answer is 2.5**

First, use distribute property to simplify $-4(x + 2)$.    $-4(x + 2) = -4x - 8$

Now, combine like terms: $x - 4(x + 2) = -15.5 \rightarrow x - 4x - 8 = -15.5 \rightarrow -3x - 8 = -15.5$

Add 8 to both sides of the equation: $-3x - 8 + 8 = -15.5 + 8 \rightarrow -3x = -7.5$. Divide both

sides by $-3$. Then: $-3x = -7.5 \rightarrow \frac{-3x}{-3} = \frac{-7.5}{-3} \rightarrow x = 2.5$

**7) Choice D is correct**

Solve for $x$. $-4 \leq 4x - 8 < 16 \Rightarrow$ Add 8 to all sides: $-4 + 8 \leq 4x - 8 + 8 < 16 + 8 \Rightarrow$

$4 \leq 4x < 24 \Rightarrow$ Divide all sides by 4: $1 \leq x < 6$

$x$ is between 1 and 6. Choice D represents this inequality.

**8) Choice D is correct**

$Volume\ of\ a\ box = length \times width \times height = 4 \times 5 \times 6 = 120$

**9) Choice A is correct**

Simplify and combine like terms. $(6x^3 - 8x^2 + 2x^4) - (4x^2 - 2x^4 + 2x^3) \rightarrow$

$(6x^3 - 8x^2 + 2x^4) - 4x^2 + 2x^4 - 2x^3 \rightarrow 4x^4 + 4x^3 - 12x^2$

**10) Choice C is correct**

the population is increased by 15% and 20%. 15% increase changes the population to 115% of original population. For the second increase, multiply the result by 120%.

$(1.15) \times (1.20) = 1.38 = 138\%$. 38 percent of the population is increased after two years.

**11) Choice C is correct**

Three times of 24,000 is 72,000. One sixth of them cancelled their tickets.

One sixth of 72,000 equals 12,000 $\left(\frac{1}{6} \times 72,000 = 12,000\right)$.

60,000 $(72,000 - 12,000 = 60,000)$ fans are attending this week

**12) The answer is 97. 6**

The area of the square is 595.36. Therefore, the side of the square is square root of the area.

$\sqrt{595.36} = 24.4$. Four times the side of the square is the perimeter: $4 \times 24.4 = 97.6$

**13) Choice D is correct**

Change the numbers to decimal and then compare.

$\frac{2}{3} = 0.666 \dots, 0.68, 67\% = 0.67, \frac{4}{5} = 0.80$

Therefore: $\frac{2}{3} < 67\% < 0.68 < \frac{4}{5}$

**14) Choice C is correct**

$$average\ (mean) = \frac{sum\ of\ terms}{number\ of\ terms} \rightarrow 88 = \frac{sum\ of\ terms}{50} \rightarrow sum = 88 \times 50 = 4,400$$

The difference of 94 and 69 is 25. Therefore, 25 should be subtracted from the sum.

$$4,400 - 25 = 4,375, mean = \frac{sum\ of\ terms}{number\ of\ terms} \rightarrow mean = \frac{4,375}{50} = 87.5$$

**15) Choice B is correct**

For sum of 5: $(1\ \&\ 4)\ and\ (4\ \&\ 1), (2\ \&\ 3)$ and $(3\ \&\ 2)$, therefore we have 4 options.

For sum of 8: $(5\ \&\ 3)\ and\ (3\ \&\ 5), (4\ \&\ 4)$ and $(2\ \&\ 6), and (6\ \&\ 2)$. There are 5 options. To get a sum of 5 or 8 for two dice: $4 + 5 = 9$

Since, we have $6 \times 6 = 36$ total number of options, the probability of getting a sum of 5 and 8 is 9 out of 36 or $\frac{9}{36} = \frac{1}{4}$

**16) The answer is 8**

Use formula of rectangle prism volume. $V = (length)(width)(height) \rightarrow$

$2,000 = (25)(10)(height) \rightarrow height = 2,000 \div 250 = 8$

**17) Choice C is correct**

To find the number of possible outfit combinations, multiply number of options for each factor:

$3 \times 5 \times 4 = 60$

**18) Choices A and B are correct**

**(If you selected 3 choices and 2 of them are correct, then you get one point. If you answered 2 or 3 choices and one of them is correct, you receive one point. If you selected more than 3 choices, you won't get any point for this question.)**

In the stadium the ratio of home fans to visiting fans in a crowd is $5:7$. Therefore, total number of fans must be divisible by $12: 5 + 7 = 12$.

Let's review the choices:

A. 12,324:     $12,324 \div 12 = 1,027$

B. 16,788:     $16,788 \div 12 = 1,399$

C. 42,326     $42,326 \div 12 = 3,527.166$

D. 44,566     $44,566 \div 12 = 3,713.833$

E. 66,812     $66,812 \div 12 = 5,567.66666$

Only choices A and B when divided by 12 result a whole number.

**19) Choice B is correct**

The diagonal of the square is 8. Let $x$ be the side.

Use Pythagorean Theorem: $a^2 + b^2 = c^2$

$x^2 + x^2 = 8^2 \rightarrow 2x^2 = 8^2 \rightarrow 2x^2 = 64 \rightarrow x^2 = 32 \rightarrow x = \sqrt{32}$

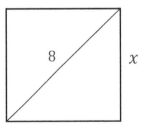

The area of the square is: $\sqrt{32} \times \sqrt{32} = 32$

**20) Choice B is correct**

$$Probability = \frac{number\ of\ desired\ outcomes}{number\ of\ total\ outcomes} = \frac{18}{12+18+18+24} = \frac{18}{72} = \frac{1}{4}$$

**21) Choices A and E are correct**

**(If you selected 3 choices and 2 of them are correct, then you get one point. If you answered 2 or 3 choices and one of them is correct, you receive one point. If you selected more than 3 choices, you won't get any point for this question.)**

$x + 2y = 4$. Plug in the values of $x$ and $y$ from choices provided. Then:

A. $(-2, 3)$      $x + 2y = 4 \rightarrow -2 + 2(3) = 4 \rightarrow -2 + 6 = 4$     This is true!

B. $(1, 2)$       $x + 2y = 4 \rightarrow 1 + 2(2) = 4 \rightarrow 1 + 4 = 5$       This is NOT true!

C. $(-1, 3)$      $x + 2y = 4 \rightarrow -1 + 2(3) = 4 \rightarrow -1 + 6 = 5$     This is NOT true!

D. $(-3, 4)$      $x + 2y = 4 \rightarrow -3 + 2(4) = 4 \rightarrow -3 + 8 = 5$     This is NOT true!

E. $(0, 2)$       $x + 2y = 4 \rightarrow 0 + 2(2) = 4 \rightarrow 4 = 4$       This is true!

**22) Choice A is correct**

The width of the rectangle is twice its length. Let $x$ be the length. Then, $width = 2x$

Perimeter of the rectangle is $2(width + length) = 2(2x + x) = 60 \rightarrow 6x = 60 \rightarrow x = 10$

Length of the rectangle is 10 meters.

**23) Choice D is correct**

$average = \dfrac{sum\ of\ terms}{number\ of\ terms} \rightarrow$

(average of 6 numbers) $12 = \dfrac{sum\ of\ numbers}{6} \rightarrow sum\ of\ 6\ numbers\ is\ 12 \times 6 = 72$

(average of 4 numbers) $10 = \dfrac{sum\ of\ numbers}{4} \rightarrow sum\ of\ 4\ numbers\ is\ 10 \times 4 = 40$

$sum\ of\ 6\ numbers - sum\ of\ 4\ numbers = sum\ of\ 2\ numbers \rightarrow 72 - 40 = 32$

$average\ of\ 2\ numbers = \dfrac{32}{2} = 16$

**24) Choice C is correct**

Solving Systems of Equations by Elimination

Multiply the first equation by $(-2)$, then add it to the second equation.

$$-2(2x + 5y = 11) \Rightarrow \begin{array}{l} -4x - 10y = -22 \\ 4x - 2y = -14 \end{array} \Rightarrow -12y = -36 \Rightarrow y = 3$$

Plug in the value of $y$ into one of the equations and solve for $x$.

$$2x + 5(3) = 11 \Rightarrow 2x + 15 = 11 \Rightarrow 2x = -4 \Rightarrow x = -2$$

**25) Choice B is correct**

The perimeter of the trapezoid is $36 \ cm$.

Therefore, the missing side (height) is $= 36 - 8 - 12 - 6 = 10$

Area of a trapezoid: $A = \frac{1}{2}h(b_1 + b_2) = \frac{1}{2}(10)(6 + 8) = 70$

**26) Choice B is correct**

The probability of choosing a Hearts is $\frac{13}{52} = \frac{1}{4}$

**27) Choices D and E are correct**

**(If you selected 3 choices and 2 of them are correct, then you get one point. If you answered 2 or 3 choices and one of them is correct, you receive one point. If you selected more than 3 choices, you won't get any point for this question.)**

First, find the sum of five numbers.

$$average = \frac{sum \ of \ terms}{number \ of \ terms} \to 25 = \frac{sum \ of \ 5 \ numbers}{5} \to sum \ of \ 5 \ numbers = 25 \times 5 = 125$$

The sum of 5 numbers is 125. If a sixth number that is greater than 42 is added to these numbers, then the sum of 6 numbers must be greater than 162. $125 + 42 = 167$

If the number was 42, then the average of the numbers is:

$$average = \frac{sum \ of \ terms}{number \ of \ terms} = \frac{167}{6} = 27.8\bar{3}$$

Since the number is bigger than 42. Then, the average of six numbers must be greater than $27.8\bar{3}$.

Choices D and E are greater than $27.8\bar{3}$.

**28) The answer is 28**

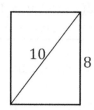

Let $x$ be the width of the rectangle. Use Pythagorean Theorem:

$$a^2 + b^2 = c^2$$

$$x^2 + 8^2 = 10^2 \Rightarrow x^2 + 64 = 100 \Rightarrow x^2 = 100 - 64 \Rightarrow x^2 = 36 \Rightarrow x = 6$$

Perimeter of the rectangle $= 2(length + width) = 2(8 + 6) = 2(14) = 28$

**29) Choice C is correct**

The ratio of boy to girls is $4 : 7$. Therefore, there are 4 boys out of 11 students. To find the answer, first divide the total number of students by 11, then multiply the result by 4. $44 \div 11 = 4 \rightarrow 4 \times 4 = 16$. There are 16 boys and 28 $(44 - 16)$ girls. So, 12 more boys should be enrolled to make the ratio $1 : 1$

**30) Choice A is correct**

2,500 out of 55,000 equals to $\dfrac{2,500}{55,000} = \dfrac{25}{550} = \dfrac{1}{22}$

**31) The answer is 60**

Jason needs an 75% average to pass for five exams. Therefore, the sum of 5 exams must be at lease $5 \times 75 = 375$. The sum of 4 exams is: $68 + 72 + 85 + 90 = 315$.

The minimum score Jason can earn on his fifth and final test to pass is: $375 - 315 = 60$

**32) Choice D is correct**

Isolate and solve for $x$. $\dfrac{2}{3}x + \dfrac{1}{6} = \dfrac{1}{3} \rightarrow \dfrac{2}{3}x = \dfrac{1}{3} - \dfrac{1}{6} \rightarrow \dfrac{2}{3}x = \dfrac{1}{6}$

Multiply both sides by the reciprocal of the coefficient of $x$. $\left(\dfrac{3}{2}\right)\dfrac{2}{3}x = \dfrac{1}{6}\left(\dfrac{3}{2}\right) \rightarrow x = \dfrac{3}{12} = \dfrac{1}{4}$

**33) Choice B is correct**

Use simple interest formula: $I = prt$ ($I$ = interest, $p$ = principal, $r$ = rate, $t$ = time)

$$I = (12,000)(0.035)(2) = 840$$

**34) Choice D is correct**

Simplify. $6x^2y^3(2x^2y)^3 = 6x^2y^3(8x^6y^3) = 48x^8y^6$

**35) Choice C is correct**

Surface Area of a cylinder $= 2\pi r(r + h)$, the radius of the cylinder is $3$ $(6 \div 2)$ inches and its height is $8$ inches. Therefore, Surface Area of a cylinder $= 2\pi(3)(3 + 8) = 66\pi\ in^2$

**36) Choice C is correct**

The square of a number is $\frac{25}{64}$, then the number is the square root of $\frac{25}{64}$. $\sqrt{\frac{25}{64}} = \frac{5}{8}$

The cube of the number is: $\left(\frac{5}{8}\right)^3 = \frac{125}{512}$

**37) Choice B is correct**

Write the numbers in order: $2, 19, 27, 28, 35, 44, 67$.

Median is the number in the middle. So, the median is $28$.

**38) The answer is 170**

Use the information provided in the question to draw the shape.

Use Pythagorean Theorem: $a^2 + b^2 = c^2$

$80^2 + 150^2 = c^2 \rightarrow 6,400 + 22,500 = c^2 \rightarrow$

$28,900 = c^2 \rightarrow c = 170$

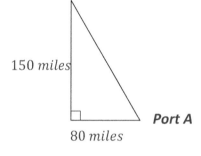

**39) Choice B is correct**

Plug in $104$ for $F$ and then solve for $C$. $C = \frac{5}{9}(F - 32) \rightarrow C = \frac{5}{9}(104 - 32) \rightarrow C = \frac{5}{9}(72) = 40$

**40) Choice C is correct**

Let $x$ be the number. Write the equation and solve for $x$.

$40\%\ of\ x = 4 \rightarrow 0.40x = 4 \rightarrow x = 4 \div 0.40 = 10$

**41) Choice D is correct**

Let $x$ be all expenses, then $\frac{22}{100}x = \$660 \rightarrow x = \frac{100 \times \$660}{22} = \$3,000$. He spent for his rent: $\frac{27}{100} \times \$3,000 = \$810$

**42) Choice C is correct**

The distance between Jason and Joe is 9 miles. Jason running at 5.5 miles per hour and Joe is running at the speed of 7 miles per hour. Therefore, every hour the distance is 1.5 miles less.

$9 \div 1.5 = 6 \; hours$

**43) Choice D is correct**

The failing rate is 11 out of $55 = \frac{11}{55}$. Change the fraction to percent: $\frac{11}{55} \times 100\% = 20\%$

20 percent of students failed. Therefore, 80 percent of students passed the exam.

**44) Choice A is correct**

First, find the number. Let $x$ be the number. Write the equation and solve for $x$.

150% of a number is 75, then: $1.5 \times x = 75 \rightarrow x = 75 \div 1.5 = 50$

90% of 50 is: $0.9 \times 50 = 45$

**45) The answer is 2**

Solve for $y$. $4x - 2y = 6 \rightarrow -2y = 6 - 4x \rightarrow y = 2x - 3$. The slope of the line is 2.

**46) Choice A is correct**

Let $x$ be the number of new shoes the team can purchase. Therefore, the team can purchase $120x$. The team had $20,000 and spent $14,000. Now the team can spend on new shoes $6,000 at most. Now, write the inequality: $120x + 14,000 \leq 20,000$

# Mathematical Reasoning Practice Test 2

## Answers and Explanations

**1) Choice C is correct**

The two greatest integers less than $-3.34$ are $-4$ and $-5$. Since $-5$ is odd, the answer is $-4$.

**2) Choice D is correct**

First draw an isosceles triangle. Remember that two sides of the triangle are equal.

Let put $a$ for the legs. Then:

$a = 8 \Rightarrow$ area of the triangle is $= \frac{1}{2}(8 \times 8) = \frac{64}{2} = 32 \; cm^2$

Isosceles right triangle

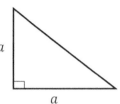

**3) Choice D is correct**

First, calcite the area of the circle and the area of the square:

Area of the circle $= \pi r^2 = \pi(6)^2 = 36\pi = 113.04 \; cm^2$

Area of the square $= 5 \; cm \times 5 \; cm = 25 \; cm^2$

To calculate the shaded area, subtract the area of the square from the area of the circle:

$113.04 \; cm^2 - 25 \; cm^2 = 88.04 \; cm^2$

**4) Choice B is correct**

The two-digit numbers must be even, so the only possible two-digit numbers must end in 6, since 6 is the only even digit given in the problem. Since the numbers cannot be repeated, the only possibilities for two-digit even numbers are 76 and 56. Thus, the answer is two possible two-digit numbers.

**5) Choice C is correct**

Since 90 boxes contain 360 $kg$ vegetable. Therefore, 1 box contains $\frac{360 \; kg}{90} = 4 \; kg$ vegetable.

**6) The answer is 144**

Let $x$ be the number: $\frac{5}{8}x = 90 \rightarrow x = 90 \times \frac{8}{5} = \frac{720}{5} = 144$

**7) The answer is 3.44**

The area of square $LMNO$ is 16 square centimeters. So:

$$S^2 = 16 \rightarrow \sqrt{S^2} = \sqrt{16} \rightarrow S = 4\ cm$$

Sides $LO$ and $NO$ are each a radius of the circle. So, the radius of the circle is $4\ cm$.

calculate the area of $\frac{1}{4}$ of the circle. The area of a circle is $A = \pi r^2$. So the area of the $\frac{1}{4}$ of the

circle, in square centimeters, is $\frac{1}{4}A = \frac{1}{4}\pi r^2 = \frac{1}{4}\pi(4)^2 = \frac{1}{4}\pi(16) = 4\pi$. For calculating the area

of shaded region, subtract area of $\frac{1}{4}$ of the circle from area of square. The area of the shaded par:

$16 - 4\pi$: and $\pi = 3.14$, then, the answer is: $16 - 4\pi = 16 - 12.56 = 3.44$

**8) Choice B is correct**

$2m = n + 5 \rightarrow m = \frac{n+5}{2}$. Substitute each value of $n$ to find the values of $m$:

$m = \frac{5+5}{2} = \frac{10}{2} = 5$

$m = \frac{3+5}{2} = \frac{8}{2} = 4$

$m = \frac{7+5}{2} = \frac{12}{2} = 6$

The set of $m$ is $\{5,4,6\}$

**9) Choice D is correct**

Let's review the choices when $x = 1$.

A. $f(x) = x^2 - 5$    if $x = 1 \rightarrow f(1) = (1)^2 - 5 = 1 - 5 = -4 \neq 5$

B. $f(x) = x^2 - 1$    if $x = 1 \rightarrow f(1) = (1)^2 - 1 = 1 - 1 = 0 \neq 5$

C. $f(x) = \sqrt{x + 2}$    if $x = 1 \rightarrow f(1) = \sqrt{1 + 2} = \sqrt{3} \neq 5$

D. $f(x) = \sqrt{x} + 4$    if $x = 1 \rightarrow f(1) = \sqrt{1} + 4 = 5$

Only choice D provides a correct answer.

**10) Choice D is correct**

Jack scored a mean of 80 per test. In the first 4 tests, the sum of scores is: $80 \times 4 = 320$. Now, calculate the mean over the 5 tests: $\frac{320+90}{5} = \frac{410}{5} = 82$

**11) Choice C is correct**

Solve for $x$: $0.00104 = \frac{104}{x}$, multiply both sides by $x$, $(0.00104)(x) = \frac{104}{x}(x)$.

Simplify: $0.00104x = 104$. Divide both side by $0.00104$: $\frac{0.00104x}{0.00104} = \frac{104}{0.00104}$, simplify

$x = \frac{104}{0.00104} = 100,000$

**12) Choice B is correct**

$(2x + 4)°$ and $96°$ are vertical angles. Vertical angles are equal in measure. Then:

$2x + 4 = 96 \rightarrow 2x = 92 \rightarrow x = 46°$

**13) Choice B is correct**

First calculate square of $-3$: $|-5| + 9 \times 2\frac{1}{3} + 9$

Convert mix number to fraction, then multiply to 9: $|-5| + \frac{63}{3} + 9$

Calculate absolute value and add terms: $5 + 21 + 9 = 35$

**14) Choice C is correct**

Use properties of equations to determine the missing expression. $\frac{2y}{x} - \frac{y}{3x} = \frac{(...)}{3x}$

$\frac{3}{3} \cdot \frac{2y}{x} - \frac{y}{3x} = \frac{(...)}{3x} \rightarrow \frac{6y}{3x} - \frac{y}{3x} = \frac{(...)}{3x} \rightarrow \frac{6y-y}{3x} = \frac{(...)}{3x} \rightarrow (...) = 5y$

**15) Choice C is correct**

Let $n$ represent a number in the sequence, and let $x$ represent the number that comes just before $n$.

$n = 4 + 2x \rightarrow 84 = 4 + 2x \rightarrow 80 = 2x \rightarrow x = 40$

**16) Choice B is correct**

Substitute 6 for $m$ and $-3$ for $n$:

$$\frac{5-9(3+n)}{3m-5(2-n)} = \frac{5-9(3+(-3))}{3(6)-5(2-(-3))} = \frac{5-9(0)}{18-5(5)} = \frac{5}{18-25} = \frac{5}{-7} = -\frac{5}{7}$$

**17) Choice A is correct**

The area of the entire circle is $\pi r^2$. The fraction of the circle that is shaded is $\frac{30}{360} = \frac{1}{12}$. So, the area of the sector is $\frac{1}{12}\pi r^2$. Use that information to find $r$.

$$\frac{1}{12}\pi r^2 = 12\pi \rightarrow r^2 = 144 \rightarrow r = 12$$

Use $r$ to calculate the circumference of the circle: $c = 2\pi r = 2\pi(12) = 24\pi$

The circumference is $24\pi$ feet.

**18) Choice B is correct**

The factors of 45 are: $\{\,1, 3, 5, 9, 15, 45\}$. Only choice B is correct.

**19) The answer is 108**

To find the number of possible outfit combinations, multiply number of options for each factor:

$6 \times 3 \times 6 = 108$

**20) The answer is 64**

The area of the circle is $16\pi$, then, its diameter is 8.

$$Area\ of\ a\ circle = \pi r^2 = 16\pi \rightarrow r^2 = 16 \rightarrow r = 4$$

Radius of the circle is 4 and diameter is twice of it, 8.

One side of the square equals to the diameter of the circle. Then:

$$Area\ of\ square = side \times side = 8 \times 8 = 64$$

**21) Choice B is correct**

First, change the improper fractions into mixed numbers: $\frac{7}{2} = 3\frac{1}{2}$ and $\frac{30}{4} = 7\frac{1}{2}$

The integers between these two values are $4, 5, 6$ and $7$. So, there are 4 integers between $\frac{7}{5}$ and $\frac{30}{4}$.

## 22) Choice D is correct

When a point is reflected over $x$ axes, the $(y)$ coordinate of that point changes to $(-y)$ while its $x$ coordinate remains the same. $C(7,9) \rightarrow C'(7,-9)$

## 23) Choice A is correct

$2x + 4 > 11x - 12.5 - 3.5x \rightarrow$ Combine like terms: $2x + 4 > 7.5x - 12.5 \rightarrow$ Subtract $2x$ from both sides: $4 > 5.5x - 12.5$. Add $12.5$ both sides of the inequality. $16.5 > 5.5x$, Divide both sides by $5.5 \rightarrow \frac{16.5}{5.5} > x \rightarrow x < 3$

## 24) Choice A is correct

Use the volume of the triangular prism formula.

$V = \frac{1}{2}(length)(base)(high) \rightarrow V = \frac{1}{2} \times 4 \times 3 \times 2 \rightarrow V = 12\ m^3$

## 25) Choice B is correct

First, list the products:

| | |
|---|---|
| $1 \times 4 = 4$ | $4 \times 5 = 20$ |
| $1 \times 6 = 6$ | $4 \times 7 = 28$ |
| $1 \times 5 = 5$ | $6 \times 5 = 30$ |
| $1 \times 7 = 7$ | $6 \times 7 = 42$ |
| $4 \times 6 = 24$ | $5 \times 7 = 35$ |

Out of 10 results, 3 numbers are odd. The answer is: $\frac{3}{10}$

## 26) Choice C is correct

Standard form of straight-line equation is: $y = mx + b$. Thus, choice C has a graph that is a straight line. All other options are not equations of straight lines.

**27) Choice B is correct**

Since $5n$ is even, then $5n + 1$ must be odd. Thus $5n + 3$ and $5n + 5$ are also odd. So, there are a total of 3 numbers in this range that are odd.

**28) Choice B is correct**

One gram is equal to 1,000 milligrams, or 1 milligram is equal to $\frac{1}{1,000}$ gram.

Thus, 85 milligrams $= \frac{85}{1,000} = 0.085$ gram

**29) Choice A is correct**

Solve for $x$: $2x - 5y = 10 \rightarrow x - \frac{5}{2}y = 5 \rightarrow x = \frac{5}{2}y + 5$

**30) Choices D and E are correct**

**(If you selected 3 choices and 2 of them are correct, then you get one point. If you answered 2 or 3 choices and one of them is correct, you receive one point. If you selected more than 3 choices, you won't get any point for this question.)**

Some of prime numbers are: $2, 3, 5, 7, 11, 13$. Find the product of two consecutive prime numbers: $2 \times 3 = 6$ (not in the options), $3 \times 5 = 15$ (bingo!), $5 \times 7 = 35$ (yes!) ,$7 \times 11 = 77$ (not in the options). Choices D and E are correct.

**31) Choice B is correct**

Since 0.0099 is equal to 0.99%, the closest to that value is 0.1%.

**32) Choice D is correct**

76% of the people polled answered yes, so 24% of the people did not answer yes. Therefore, 66 people is 24% of the total, $x$.

$\frac{66}{x} = \frac{24}{100} \rightarrow \frac{66}{x} = \frac{6}{25} \rightarrow 66(25) = 6x \rightarrow \frac{66(25)}{6} = x \rightarrow x = 275$

**33) The answer is 45**

Perimeter of figure $A$ is: $2\pi r = 2\pi \frac{10}{2} = 10\pi = 10 \times 3 = 30$

Area of figure $B$ is: $6 \times 10 = 60$, $Average = \frac{30 + 60}{2} = \frac{90}{2} = 45$

**34) The answer is 46.26**

Given diameter $= 18\ cm \rightarrow$ radius $= 9cm$

Perimeter of circle $= 2\pi r = 2 \times \pi \times 9 = 18\pi = 56.52\ cm$

The perimeter of semi−circular slice is:

$P = \frac{perimeter\ of\ circle}{2} + 2r = \frac{56.52}{2} + 2(9) = 46.26\ cm$

**35) Choice B is correct**

Set up a proportion to solve.

$\frac{1\frac{1}{7}in}{\frac{1}{5}yr} = \frac{x\ in}{1\ yr} \rightarrow 1\frac{1}{7} = \frac{1}{5}x \rightarrow \frac{8}{7} = \frac{1}{5}x \rightarrow \left(\frac{5}{1}\right)\left(\frac{8}{7}\right) = x \rightarrow \frac{40}{7} = x \rightarrow x = 5\frac{5}{7}$

**36) Choice B is correct**

Let $x$ be the number of inches representing 2.5 feet. Set up a proportion and solve for $x$:

$\frac{x}{2.5} = \frac{0.15}{150} \rightarrow x = \frac{0.15 \times 2.5}{150} \rightarrow x = 0.0025\ in$

**37) Choice D is correct**

Set an equation: $\frac{3}{7}Z = 54$

Solve for $Z$: $Z = 54 \times \frac{7}{3} = 126$, then calculate $\frac{2}{5}Z$: $\frac{2}{5} \times 126 = 50.4$

**38) Choice D is correct**

The spent amount is \$60 and the tip is 25%. Then: $tip = 0.25 \times 60 = \$15$

$Final\ price = Selling\ price + tip \rightarrow final\ price = \$60 + \$15 = \$75$

**39) Choice D is correct**

To find the smallest factor of 95, list the factors: $1, 5, 19,$ and $95.$ The smallest factor (other than 1) is 5. Of the choices listed $(28, 32, 39,$ and $45)$, only 45 is a multiple of 5.

**40) Choice A is correct**

Adding exponents is done by calculating each exponent first and then adding and dividing:

$\frac{4^2+3^2+(-5)^2}{(9+10-11)^2} = \frac{16+9+25}{(8)^2} = \frac{50}{64} = \frac{25}{32}$

**41) Choice B is correct**

Angle $A$ and angle $B$ are supplementary, so the sum of their angles is $180°$.

Let $a$ equal the measure of angle $A$, and let $b$ equal the measure of angle $B$. $a + b = 180$

The measure of angle $A$ is 2 times the measure of angle $B$.

$$a = 2b \rightarrow 2b + b = 180 \rightarrow 3b = 180 \rightarrow b = \frac{180}{3} = 60 \rightarrow a = 2b = 2(60) = 120$$

Therefore, the measure of angle $A$ is $120°$.

**42) Choice D is correct**

$$3\frac{1}{4} + 2\frac{4}{16} + 1\frac{3}{8} + 5\frac{1}{2}$$

Convert all the fractions to a common denominator:

$$3\frac{4}{16} + 2\frac{4}{16} + 1\frac{6}{16} + 5\frac{8}{16} = (3 + 2 + 1 + 5) + \left(\frac{4+4+6+8}{16}\right) = 11 + 1\frac{6}{16} = 12\frac{6}{16} = 12\frac{3}{8}$$

**43) Choices B and E are correct**

**(If you selected 3 choices and 2 of them are correct, then you get one point. If you answered 2 or 3 choices and one of them is correct, you receive one point. If you selected more than 3 choices, you won't get any point for this question.)**

There are 60 seconds in 1 minute. Divide the number of seconds by the number of second in 1 minute: $\frac{9,000}{60} = 150$ minutes or 2.5 hours.

**44) Choice D and E are correct**

**(If you selected 3 choices and 2 of them are correct, then you get one point. If you answered 2 or 3 choices and one of them is correct, you receive one point. If you selected more than 3 choices, you won't get any point for this question.)**

Simplify the inequality: $2y + 6 < 30 \rightarrow 2y < 30 - 6 \rightarrow 2y < 24 \rightarrow y < 12$. Only choices D (8) and E ($-12$) are less than 12.

**45) Choice C is correct**

The first integer is $m$, so the second is $m + 1$, the rest are $m + 2, m + 3, m + 4, m + 5, m + 6$ and finally $m + 7$. Since $n$ is the eight and greatest of the integers, $n = m + 7$.

Substitute $m + 7$ for $n$ and simplify: $\frac{m+n}{3} = \frac{m+m+7}{3} = \frac{2m+7}{3}$

**46) Choice C is correct**

There are 6 spaces, so first divide 140 by 6: $140 \div 6 = 23$ remainder 2. So, the arrow goes around 23 full circle and then 2 more spaces. Two spaces from Space $O$ is Space $Q$.

... So Much More Online!

Effortless Math Online GED Math Center offers a complete study program, including the following:

- ✓ Step-by-step instructions on how to prepare for the GED Math test

- ✓ Numerous GED Math worksheets to help you measure your math skills

- ✓ Complete list of GED Math formulas

- ✓ Video lessons for GED Math topics

- ✓ Full-length GED Math practice tests

- ✓ And much more...

**No Registration Required.**

Visit **EffortlessMath.com/GED** to find your online GED Math resources.

# The Best GED Math Books!

## Download eBooks (in PDF format) Instantly!

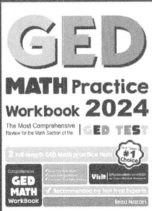

## This perfect bundle contains

✓ GED Math for Beginners 2024
✓ GED Math Practice Workbook 2024
✓ GED Math Full Study Guide 2024-2025
✓ GED Math IN 10 Days!

Visit www.EffortlessMath.com
for Online Math Practic

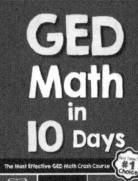

Reza Nazari

download at

**Download**

# Most Popular GED Math Books!

# 10 Full-Length GED Math Practice Tests

**The Practice You Need to Ace the GED Math Test**

Download at

**Download**

# GED Math Exercise Book

**A Comprehensive Workbook + GED Math Practice Tests 2024**

Download at

**Download**

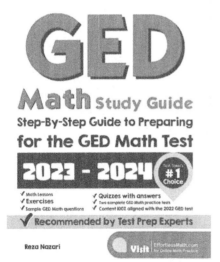

# GED Math Study Guide

**Step-By-Step Guide to Preparing for the GED Math Test**

**2023 - 2024**

Download at

**Download**

# GED Math Test Prep 2024

**The Ultimate Guide to GED Math + 2 Full-Length Practice Tests**

Download at

**Download**

# Receive the PDF version of this book or get another FREE book!

Thank you for using our Book!

Do you LOVE this book?

Then, you can get the PDF version of this book or another book absolutely FREE!

Please email us at:

info@EffortlessMath.com

for details.

# Author's Final Note

I hope you enjoyed reading this book. You've made it through the book! Great job!

First of all, thank you for purchasing this practice book. I know you could have picked any number of books to help you prepare for your GED Math test, but you picked this book and for that I am extremely grateful.

It took me years to write this workbook for the GED Math because I wanted to prepare a comprehensive GED Math workbook to help test takers make the most effective use of their valuable time while preparing for the test.

After teaching and tutoring math courses for over a decade, I've gathered my personal notes and lessons to develop this practice book. It is my greatest hope that the exercises in this book could help you prepare for your test successfully.

If you have any questions, please contact me at reza@effortlessmath.com and I will be glad to assist. Your feedback will help me to greatly improve the quality of my books in the future and make this book even better. Furthermore, I expect that I have made a few minor errors somewhere in this book. If you think this to be the case, please let me know so I can fix the issue as soon as possible.

If you enjoyed this book and found some benefit in reading this, I'd like to hear from you and hope that you could take a quick minute to post a review on the book's Amazon page. To leave your valuable feedback, please visit: amzn.to/3sid5qa

Or scan this QR code.

I personally go over every single review, to make sure my books really are reaching out and helping students and test takers. Please help me help GED Math test takers, by leaving a review!

I wish you all the best in your future success!


**Reza Nazari**

**Math teacher and author**

Made in the USA
Monee, IL
25 October 2024

68629716R00116